Responding To The Call

Responding To The Call

A guidebook to acquaint you with vortex energy

**By
Sharon Marer, M.S.
and
Shirley Piwonski**

Compiled By
Shirley Piwonski

Sources of Light Publishing
P.O. Box 6193
Aloha, Oregon 97007

First Edition, 1994

© Kindred Friends, 1994

All rights reserved: No part of this book, either in part or in whole, may be reproduced, transmitted or utilized in any form or by any means, electronic, photographic or mechanical, including photocopying, recording or by any information storage and retrieval system, without permission in writing from the publisher, except for brief quotations embodied in literary articles and reviews. Permission is not needed for recording the meditations if for personal use.

Liability Waiver: Due to the possibility of mental or emotional stress from working with vortex energy, the authors and publisher accept no responsibility for the outcome of such to any person using this book. The authors and publisher also accept no responsibility for any physical discomfort or injury due to walking the vortexes described in this book.

ISBN 1-885782-89-6

Photographs:
Front cover taken by Shirley Piwonski
Page 51 taken by Karen Ball
Pages 106, 142, taken by Dana Allen
Back cover, pages 27, 100, 114, taken by Karen VanDomelen
All remaining photographs taken by Shirley Piwonski

Dedication:

We dedicate this book to the wise,
old spirit that recognized
our hidden potential.

Acknowledgments:

We wish to thank our fellow journey friends for their descriptive quotes presented throughout this book: Marcy, Jeanine, Phil, Dave, Tara, Rebecca, David, Karen, Anne, Phillip, Lucy, Norm, Sue, Joe, Dan, Justin and Tessa.

We also want to thank Trish Rainey-Smith for her eagle eyes that brought form and continuity to this book through the editing process.

And finally, our thanks go to all the beautiful journey friends and family who believed in what we were creating and trusted enough to walk with us into the unknown.

Table of Contents

Preface i

Directions 1

Introduction to
Sedona and the Vortexes 11

Airport Mesa 21

Bell Rock 45

Cathedral Rock 67
    (Back O'Beyond) 69
    (Red Rock Crossing) 93

Boynton Canyon 113
    Kachina Woman 131

Schnebly Hill 141

Conclusion 171

More Information About...
    What To Bring 175
    Proper Breathing 178
    The Chakra System 179
    Dreams and Vortex Energy 182
    Animals on the Vortexes 187
    Stewardship 195
    Definitions 197

References 203
About the Authors 205
Index 207

Preface

"Let's go to Sedona!" And one week later we were off. Impulsive? Perhaps, but we had heard the call of the vortexes and we were compelled to respond. Some listen to the call for years before they make their first journey. Others hear it and go immediately.

We awoke a whirlwind within ourselves. Our lives changed, not the day we arrived in Sedona, but the day we made the commitment to go. We felt anxiety because of the investment of time, energy and money into a trip that had not yet defined itself. We did not know what we would do there or even why we were going. We gathered our experiences, resources and sense of adventure and set off for Arizona.

During the trip, questions began to surface. Why are we going? What will we do? What is a vortex? Are there really space people there? What about the dolphins we keep hearing about? Why are the rocks red? How does this place enhance psychic energy? How do we find the vortexes and know that we are at the right spot?

We were exuberant upon our arrival in Phoenix. Not realizing that we were already on our journey of change, we had car rental adventures, we took wrong turns on the freeways, and a camper full of kids blew a tire in front of us while doing 65 miles an hour. Were we aware yet of what we were into? No. We were excited, curious, and not at all in touch with the reality of Sedona or what vortex energy was.

We went directly to Bell Rock before going into the town of Sedona. We literally ran up the rock and began to explore. The visit was short and we decided to return later so that we could watch the sun set. We thought it would be such fun to watch the sun go down from Bell. When we returned, we began to channel information so as to learn all we could about the area and the vortexes.

Time slipped away, the sun set and we were still engrossed in the learning process. We would have continued, oblivious to the darkness, if it had not been for a rattlesnake expressing his dismay at our presence on his turf. The piercing noise of the rattle vibrated within us; we had our hearts in our throats. The reality of the moment was shocking. There was a rattler only a few feet from us, it was getting quite dark, and we were not sure of the trail back to the car. In a flash, we gathered our belongings and stuffed them into our backpacks. It seemed as if we were moving at the speed of light. We began the descent off Bell and discovered that we were in a very dangerous situation.

The energy of Bell was changing with the setting of the sun. Our ability to recognize where we were was distorted. Fear began to grip, and the distortion grew. Drop offs appeared at every turn and we had only a small penlight between the two of us. It felt as if we were caught in a black maze in which every turn held danger. We decided to take a break, calm ourselves and try to intuit where we were and how to safely descend. Calmed, we slowly and steadfastly made our way down.

Upon arrival at the bottom of Bell, we still had to find our way to the car; that became round two of our journey into darkness with Bell. The area around Bell is covered with juniper six feet tall as well as a great deal of scrub brush which we had to make our way through. We never found the trail to our car but instead ended up blazing our own. We walked toward the sounds of traffic and the guiding lights of the passing cars. We wandered around for quite some time until, off in the distance, we saw the road, whereupon we started to relax and our nerves began to settle. We let go of our fears and laughed. We completely forgot our predicament and began to think about other things, such as where do we go for dinner.

Suddenly, a strange sense of foreboding fell over us and we stopped in our tracks. Looking down, we saw the road fifteen feet below us. We were dumbfounded and our bodies went numb. Where did this drop off come from? We did not remember anything like this. It was flat where we had parked the car.

Confused, we felt as if we had entered some kind of time warp or altered reality. It was very difficult to think logically or clearly. We were in shock. What had happened to us? Were we going to live through this? Is Sedona really a good idea? After resting a moment and again collecting ourselves we tried to locate the car. It was not visible and we had no idea where we were in regards to where it was parked. Our internal compasses were spinning wildly.

Realizing that our adventure was not over, we dismissed our dinner plans and tried to assess the situation. We had been prematurely confident that we were safe and had not considered any potential danger.

We decided to pay close attention to every step we took. We did not linger on thoughts of tarantulas or snakes in the brush that we were walking through. Following the edge of the drop off, we blindly walked where our senses guided us, and finally stumbled onto the car.

It took us about three hours. We knew that we had walked the darkness of old. We gained a great deal of respect for Bell, vortex energy, and sunsets in Sedona. We now only visit the vortexes at night that we know will be safe after dark. We also bring big flashlights with us so that we will have a peaceful and safe sunset experience. Any time we drive by Bell after dark and see any cars in the parking area, we remember our treacherous time and send prayers to those still there.

It was not until after our first experience on Bell Rock that we realized that we had better come down from the clouds and examine what was in front of us.  Sedona was truly unlike any place that we had been to before. Every event had meaning and ideas emerged from places unknown. We observed others, as well as ourselves, to analyze what was happening. We saw people share with friends, meditate, write in their diaries, chant, sing, and even cry. We also observed people walk around as if they were searching for something.

We recognized that each vortex was different. As we went deeper into ourselves and the energy, these differences began to emerge. For example, that which surfaced at Bell was very intense compared to Airport. Movement was essential at Airport but in contrast, stillness was required at Cathedral Rock.

Eventually we discovered that our talents harmonized with each other and soon we were able to flow with each vortex and feel what it touched in us. We felt that we could create a plan of personal change and use vortex energy to facilitate those changes. As we worked with the energy, others began to ask how they too could access the vortex energy. We began to envision how valuable it would be to have vortex energy come alive in people, and thus we created what we call "Journeys".

Journey friends in morning check in groups

We facilitated groups of people to find a connection to the vortexes and through that connection, incredible life changes have happened. Jeanine, a coffee shop owner, remembers "I had the feeling of being a small lizard expanding to being a part of everything, each and every person. My heart chakra opened and the love was tremendous! I have only to think of Sedona and I again feel the expansion and love."

As our vision manifested, we saw dramatic shifts in people. Their lives changed before our eyes, and our lives changed along with theirs. We knew that we had created a good process. It opened people to their blocks and fears and to a beliefs in their hopes and dreams.

Next, we wanted to create a real and practical way to work with vortex energy that would touch many people. We envisioned people able to go to Sedona and tap into that energy on their own. That vision is now alive in your hands; this book "Sedona, Responding to the Call." Live the vision in yourself. Happy Journey.

Trail into Boynton Canyon

Directions to Airport Mesa

You will be looking for Airport Road, which is one mile from the intersection of Hwys. 89A and 179. You will head West at the "Y" towards Cottonwood. Turn left onto Airport Road and go approximately 1/2 mile. You will see a parking area on your left and if you come to a cattle guard, you have gone too far. Be considerate of others when parking your car. It is a small parking area, and many people come here.

Airport Mesa Vista

Go straight up the mountain at the parking lot. You will see a clearing as you look at the mountain from the parking lot. This spot is the most visited area of Airport Mesa. The panorama from this spot contains Chimney Rock, Capital Butte and Coffeepot Rock to the North. To the Northeast you will see Wilson and Munds Mountains.

Medicine Wheel Area

Once out of your car, look for a trailhead, to the left as you are facing the rocks. The trail follows the road for a short distance. Stay near the road until you see it move gracefully up the hill. This trail will take you up the mountain quite comfortably.

When you come to a clearing at the top of the mountain, look for a trail that goes off to the left as you are looking out at the horizon. It will take you around to a medicine wheel. As of the printing of this book, the wheel is still there, but there is no guarantee that it will still exist when you visit. You will know that you are in the right area by the exquisite view of Courthouse, Bell and Cathedral Rocks. This area is less visited, and, therefore a little more private.

One note of caution! As you are walking towards the medicine wheel area, the trail gets a little steep and close to the edge. Be very careful when walking it. If you have a fear of heights, or of being too close to an edge, you may not want to attempt this trail. We are telling you of this area because of the magnificent view and the energy that seems to be present here.

Directions to Cathedral Rock

Cathedral is huge and there are many ways to enjoy it. The following are three options to areas that you can explore.

Option One: Back O'Beyond Road

From the junction of Hwys. 89A and 179 in Sedona, go south approximately 3 miles to Back O'Beyond Road. Turn right onto the dirt road. Follow this road for .8 miles until you come to a small parking lot to the left. You will see a sign that says "Last Turn Around for Non-Residential Traffic." Park in the lot and proceed up to Cathedral Rock, which will be in front of you. There are trails that will lead you to the base of Cathedral. Please stay on the trails so that you will not harm the vegetation in the area. If it starts to rain, get off Cathedral immediately, as it is a flash flood area.

Option Two: Verde Valley Road

From Sedona, on Hwy. 179, go south to the Village of Oak Creek. You will turn right onto Verde Valley Rd. It is approximately 7 miles from the intersection of Hwys. 179 and 89A. Go approximately 5 miles and you will see a parking lot on your left. Walk .2 miles along the road and you will come to Oak Creek. (The other side of the river is Red Rock Crossing.) From here, look for trails or clearings that will lead you to the base of Cathedral. If it starts to rain get off Cathedral Rock.

Option Three: Red Rock Crossing

Go west on Hwy. 89A toward Cottonwood, which is approximately 3.8 miles from the "Y" intersection of Hwys. 89A and 179 in Sedona. Turn left onto Upper Red Rock Loop Road. Stay alert because the road is not very visible.

Follow the signs to Red Rock Crossing. Park only in the designated areas. This area is well patrolled, and you could get a ticket for illegal parking. The park has been improved with more parking and picnic tables. They are charging a fee to use the park facilities and this area is very full on weekends. If you choose to go on a weekend, be sure and get there early. Once parked you are close to the swimming and picnic area. Grab your towel and inner tube and jump in!

Also, if you cross the river, you will find a trail that will guide you up the face of Cathedral Rock.

Directions To Bell Rock

Bell Rock is located on Hwy. 179, near the Village of Oak Creek. As you are heading towards Sedona, from Phoenix, it will be on your right side. There are pull offs near Bell. You will know Bell Rock by its bell shape. You will also see it, in the distance, long before you actually reach it. There is no mistaking Bell Rock.

If you are coming from Sedona, Bell is approximately 5.1 miles from the junctions of Hwys. 89A and 179 and it will be on your left.

There are two parking areas about a block apart. One of these pull out areas does not have direct access to Bell. Coming from Phoenix, the turnout you want to park at is the first turnout on the right. Coming from Sedona, it is the second turnout on your left.

Once parked, you will see a wonderful trail, marked with stones, that will take you right up to the front side of Bell. From here you can explore and find the area that is most comfortable for you. If you walked around to the side of Bell closest to Courthouse Rock, you would find it a little more private. The energy of Bell here is quiet and very conducive to introspection.

Leave Bell a minimum of one hour before sunset on any day because the energy changes and can cause you much disorientation and confusion. Bell is treacherous when dusk hits.

Directions To Boynton Canyon and Kachina Woman

An easy way to find Boynton Canyon is to follow the signs that take you to "Enchantment Resort," These directions begin at Dry Creek Road. Park in the parking lot to the right just before you reach "Enchantment." You will find Boynton Canyon trail FS #47 here.

Or you can use the following directions:

Traveling west on Hwy. 89A, towards Cottonwood, you will come to Dry Creek Road, which is approximately 3 miles from the intersection of Hwys. 89A and 179. Turn right. On Dry Creek Road, you will go approximately 2.8 miles to a "T" intersection in the road. Turn left onto Boynton Pass Rd. and follow the road about 1.6 miles until you come to another "T" in the road. At this point, turn right onto Boynton Canyon Rd. and proceed to a parking lot on the right. You will see the gate to Enchantment from the parking lot.

Once parked, you will find Boynton Canyon Trail FS #47. You can take this trail into the extension of the canyon if you go to the left. Also from the parking lot you will see Kachina Woman off to the right. Take a trail that will keep moving up towards her, if this is where you want to go. Although there is a trail, it can be difficult. It also takes you through much brush and bramble. When you get near Kachina, it is somewhat difficult to find an open spot to stop and blend into the energy.

In spite of all the obstacles, Kachina is a wonderful place to launch your prayers of hope for your visions. It is awe inspiring to feel the energy of peacefulness. It is a wonderful place of physical symbols. If you choose to not hike into Kachina, you can stay near the parking lot and still launch your prayers. You will still put forth your vision and receive any information that Kachina may choose to give to you.

If you are not comfortable with a slightly difficult walk, do not attempt it. We take no responsibility for what you choose to do and any outcome from that choice.

To find another part of Boynton Canyon, look to the right of FS #47 and walk around Kachina Woman. The trail follows the phone lines.

Directions To Schnebly Hill

Leaving Sedona heading south on Hwy. 179, take a left onto Schnebly Hill Road. Immediately on turning, set your odometer to "0." Go 3.5 miles up the road. As you approach the vortex area, you will see a slight clearing with a large flat rock on the right. (Do not expect to see any specific landmarks to show you that you are in the right spot.) The trail that you will be using is on the left side of the road. You may want to turn around and park on the side where the trail is on. Once on the trail, you will come across a small area of trees, walk through the trees and when you come to a clearing you will be where the vortex energy begins.

Introduction

To Sedona and the Vortexes

The town of Sedona, named after Sedona Schnebly, one of the first white settlers in this area in 1902, is located in central Arizona, has a population of 15,000+ and is approximately 4500 feet in elevation. Sedona has become a mecca, not only of spiritual seekers, but also for lovers of the arts or those seeking retirement in their golden years. It is a picturesque community that has attracted people from all walks of life and generations.

Sedona, Arizona

Before Sedona was founded, this area was the land of, first, the Sinagua and then the Yavapai Indians. The Ancient Ones, the Sinagua (500-1400) and then the Yavapai (1500-1875) held the Sedona area as sacred and knew of its specialness. Both used it as a place of connection with the Great Spirit. They knew that it enhanced one's visions and abilities to explore one's true purpose and meaning of life. The red rocks held the power to stimulate thoughts as well as the physical body and, therefore, became the place for ceremonies and rituals.

The Sinagua lived in the canyons around Sedona and not necessarily on the vortexes or the sacred spots. The Yavapai were wanderers and ranged over an immense area using the Sedona area only for ceremony. With the coming of the white settlers, the land changed and the Yavapai, under the orders of General Crook, were marched to the Fort McDowell Reservation. It was a brutal and aggressive march and was known as the "March of Tears." More information about the native people of this area can be found in "Sedona - Sacred Earth" by Nicholas R. Mann. It helps to understand the chronology of life in this area and how the vortex energy was unique and special long ago.

So, what exactly is vortex energy and how does one work effectively with that energy? It is similar to a cyclone or whirlwind of energy. Electric vortex energy spirals up from the ground into the universe. It is masculine in nature and stimulates our emotional as well as physical aspects. Magnetic vortex energy flows from the top of the rocks down into the earth and back out again. It is feminine in nature and stimulates our inner subconscious self. It also enhances our abilities to receive. Electro-Magnetic energy is a combination of both within a specific area which creates a self balance.

A vortex creates a circle of energy and intensifies whatever you feel or believe during that specific time. It increases your vibrational flow because you are in the center of this flow. Therefore, you are effected by its touch. There are advantages to presenting yourself to this kind of intense energy. It awakens the unconscious and the unknown. You begin to transform yourself into that which you wish to be by getting a kind of "kick start". Many people do not know how to work with this energy, and therefore do not receive the full benefit.

It is very difficult to describe energy because it cannot be seen, and unless you are very sensitive and aware, it cannot be felt. Whether you feel vortex energy or not, it does exist in our world. It influences us in ways we do not always comprehend. For example, you are in a conversation with friends and they are sharing their encounters with vortex energy while in Sedona, Arizona, and your body shudders. They explain how unusual they felt while in that particular area. Among other things, they recognized their psychic abilities were heightened and that they seemed to lose track of time.

They found it a very powerful experience. In analyzing how they felt, they noticed a difference between Bell Rock and Cathedral Rock. They learned that Bell was an electric energy, which felt like a spiraling beacon of light, while Cathedral was a magnetic energy, which felt like a waterfall of velvet rays enveloping them.

You next encounter your friend's pictures of the immense red rock formations, and that same shudder engulfs you. You begin to wonder: what is beckoning me? The call of the vortex energy, through the red rocks, is often intriguing, awakening within you the desire to explore the mysteries of life. You may not always understand why you are called by these mystical forces, but a metamorphosis within you has already begun. Your journey of change is unfolding.

You have an awareness of the need for change within you. You see aspects of your life where changes become significant, and you explore how to make these changes happen. Once the desire for change has been identified, accept the help being offered through the mystical call of the vortexes.

Each vortex is different. For example, Bell Rock is a physical energy and should be worked from that perspective. Bell works with action and movement through release. Because it is a place of doing, the energy of Bell helps the hidden surface. We can then begin to process this information. Physical exercises, which bring one in touch with the physical self, may enhance your time there.

Bell Rock is an electric energy center. Here, your body senses something different, a charged current of energy speeding through, taking with it old, as well as present physical and emotional pains, along with ancient and ancestral wounds. This is where unconscious stirrings rise to consciousness. You may find yourself agitated, yet exhilarated. Physical as well as emotional sensations become more defined. Through the agitation, you will be able to attain an expanded inner truth.

Airport Mesa, also an electric energy center, is a wonderful launching point for your search into yourself. Once in this electric energy, you need to have a heartfelt purpose, or desire, which will help you tap into the whirlpool of energy. To totally experience this vortex identify exactly where you are in your life and you will be able to move into motion. Airport Mesa, through accepting change, launches a new viewpoint along your journey of life. It gently helps you to see life in its reality, with the awareness that there is hope for change. Within this vortex, one begins to feel as if he can accomplish exactly what he is setting out to do.

The mystical call of Sedona could easily draw you to Cathedral Rock, a magnetic vortex. Through magnetic energy, introspection and knowledge come together. The essence of this energy is far more gentle and heartfelt than that found within the electric vortexes. Serenity is cradled within the pinnacles of Cathedral. When visiting the pinnacles, you move into a state of quiet, which allows you to receive the love knowledge and opens your intuitive channels. Through this intuitive energy, you begin to communicate from within. Symbols and feelings are presented, bringing awareness of what one has received. Cathedral produces a desire to go inward and explore the self. You may not feel this energy through your physical body, but it draws information from your unconscious into your conscious mind.

Cathedral Rock from Back O'Beyond Rd.

Past issues, long forgotten, but still affecting you, may surface. You may be rather surprised to feel them surface because you may have considered these issues to be resolved. Cathedral lets you know that they need to be reexamined. Cathedral is a place of self reflection where abilities of intuition are enhanced and then expressed.

Another major vortex is Boynton Canyon, an electro-magnetic energy. As a blend of the electric and magnetic, it creates balance. It makes real the symbols and intuitive knowledge received. The energy is accessed by simply walking the canyon. Each person will find different realizations while on his walk. You may find the freedom to be yourself, or let go of your fears so as to evaluate your life. This final type of vortex energy is very powerful because it shows you how to live. It helps you celebrate life by gently connecting you to your world.

Although not yet called a vortex, but becoming very popular is Schnebly Hill, which has a strong electro-magnetic energy of a universal nature. It is very seventh chakra, in that it seems to pull you out into the universe. It is wonderful for physical and emotional healing because it brings issues forward from a holistic perspective; it presents a whole self picture. You feel "God" energy here.

Through accepting the wisdom given to you, through your exploration of each of the vortexes, you become aware that you have the choice, as well as the ability, to walk free of the old ways of seeing and living. You begin to integrate knowledge received with the desire to walk life with fulfillment and awareness. You have self-awareness releasing that which no longer fits, and filling yourself with clarity of purpose and a desire to continue your walk.

The energy of the vortexes is very different from what you experience in everyday life. For example, time is difficult to track. The desire for food is greatly lessened and you may lose your appetite. You may find it difficult to grasp and hold ideas that come to you. Verbalizing helps, but it is better to write ideas down or use a tape recorder. Your heart rate may be different. Your limbs may unexpectedly experience pain or tightness. In moments of release, shift, or change, you may feel intense heat, which is a connection to the vortex energy of release. Headaches occur with the lightening of the crown chakra, allowing you to astrally connect with the vortexes to acquire physical release, new knowledge, or a lightening of yourself.

The physical sensations are a necessary part of vortex learning, although not everyone chooses to utilize vortex vibration for release and change. If you do choose these purposes, the energy will move through you and you will feel the physical sensations. Issues held in the body will be affected by the vibration. You are touching cellular memory every time you connect to vortex energy.

Vortex energy is not yet completely understood. It is very complex. The energy encourages physical release because it moves into and through the body. The chakras in the feet and palms open when you start to walk through vortex energy. The energy gathers in all of the major chakras and moves up and out through the crown. As you walk on the vortexes you can feel the energy as it covers your body.

Sleep habits change. You may either have very vivid dreams, or find it difficult to sleep at all. Even if you do not sleep very well, you may find that you are still refreshed in the morning.

You can gain a great deal of insight through your dreams. They contain additional information for you about your time spent with the vortexes. Write down your dreams as you awaken each morning, as they easily slip away as we begin our busy days. Look for symbols hidden within your dreams as well as any connections to your present life. Take your written dreams to the vortexes and ask for guidance as to their meaning. Because the vortexes enhance meditations, you could, while in a meditative state, either draw the symbols or write down anything that comes to you about your dreams. Examine what you have written once you complete the meditation. The vortexes bring forth, in most people, the desire to sit and meditate, which is a very valuable way to introduce yourself to the vortex energy. However, one should not stop at meditation to get the full benefit of the energy.

A quiet moment on Bell Rock

The time spent in the vortexes is very moving. You may find yourself with emotional feelings such as anger, joy, and fear and not know what to do with those feelings. Getting in touch with vortex energy is a very transformational experience. Accept whatever is presented. If the emotions or feelings are uncomfortable, try to write down what you are experiencing. Look deep into the feelings and what they could mean to you. Often these feelings help us to discover ourselves.

Each vortex is special in what it shares with us. Each person responds differently to each vortex. However, do not visit one vortex after another without "washing" the energy of the first off your body. While on a vortex, you are breathing in the energy surrounding your body. When you leave, you take this energy with you. It is necessary to wash that vortex off your body before visiting the next. The blending of very different energies causes irritation or emotional imbalance. A shower, a swim, or even a hot tub leaves you feeling refreshed and clear to experience another vortex.

You may favor one vortex over another, and this is good information for you about yourself. Some people are "space" or physically oriented, and will be drawn to Bell Rock. You may be ready to release physical blocks and the energy of Bell will help. You may be intuitive, and find yourself engulfed in the magic of Cathedral Rock. You may prefer the balanced earthy vibration of Boynton Canyon, or the totality and healing vibration of Schnebly Hill. One vortex is not better than another. Each is special unto itself.

Airport Mesa

*The Place of the Night Fire:
the beginning of the quest*

The invitation to Airport Mesa begins as you drive up a meandering hill. It seems as if the heavens are welcoming you and you are full of anticipation upon your arrival. Look around. You feel sensitive and alert to something important happening. Park your car and look directly at the bluff ahead of you. Is this where the call wants to take you?

In a sense of wonder, you realize that there is an inviting trail to the east of the bluff*. You feel the need for movement and head towards the trail. The walk along the trail becomes quieter and quieter and your pace takes on a meditative rhythm.

The path enters a clearing and then continues up and along the ridge of the mountain. You are filled with that sense of being drawn upward, as well as a sense of

* *As you look at the bluff from the parking lot the trail is to the left.*

anticipation. As you make your way around the ledge, you are greeted by the medicine wheel and a view that is heart rendering; a panoramic picture vibrating with energy and stunning vistas in every direction. You sense the gripping charge of Bell Rock's energy as you gaze at it in the western sky. The serene mystique of Cathedral, which is to the right of Bell, adds to the immenseness of this view. The stateliness of Courthouse Rock, on Bell's left, fills you with quiet reverence. It feels as if this is an incredible center point or gathering hub of energies. The greeting opens your heart. You feel the touch, something has begun.

What you feel at Airport changes as the morning slips into night. The early morning hours present a feeling of waking up after a good night's sleep. It is peaceful and serene as the sun begins to rise. Breathing in the energy is like having your morning cup of coffee. You slowly start to wake up to the day, or to the things you want to search about yourself. As you breathe, you are taking in the energy of this vortex and you begin your connection to it.

As the sun rises, so does the intensity of the energy and it takes on momentum as the hours pass. Some feel it as a kick start or a motivating force. As you take in the energy, realize that you are filling up with an energy that induces movement and change. You will notice your body talking to you here because you are making a connection to the earth through your body.

You feel the neutralizing, balancing, electric vibration as it spirals up from the ground into the heavens. This is the place where simplicity of life begins to take on strength. You let go of the complicated, the not understood and just let yourself be in the moment and in the energy around you. Here, the energies present a communication of pictures, symbols, and words that you will understand. You may feel as if issues inside are beginning to erupt or require definition.

It is preferable to release excess baggage on one visit and create future plans on the next. Life can not be lived without meaning or purpose. We need a purpose, a heartfelt purpose, when visiting the vortexes. Airport enhances the feeling of trying to find that purpose. Because of the nature of the energy here, the morning hours open up the opportunity to reach into the self, and that opportunity keeps building as the day progresses. But as the day slips into night, a new energy begins to envelop the area.

Sunsets in Sedona are spectacular. The blazing red sun fills the sky as it begins its descent into the horizon. As night pushes the sun into slumber, it reminds us of a blazing campfire licking at the darkness. The flames provocatively dance us into ourselves. As the night sky is performing this dance, the earth becomes its dance partner, and the darkness embraces the night fire. The vortex power awakens with an intensity similar to kundalini power, meaning that it awakens the belief in our own abilities and that we can achieve our goals. We feel power-full and bring forth the courage to search deeper into our fears. We also use that same courage to accept our strengths.

Dave from Portland, Oregon, found Airport "agitating, because it shakes things up. It's illusive, it's a game to touch it. It's chaotic, and seems to peak in the afternoon. I like it at night because the edge is off. It's fascinating in the evenings. When I walked to Airport in the evenings, I could see a flame torching up from spots in the ground. They were like torches of flames erupting from the ground. I can see why this is the place of the night fire."

At Airport, you may notice that as you put out your hands near the edge of the cliff, you feel the energy pushing back. This sensation, along with the immense, breathtaking view, leads you to believe that you could accomplish anything. That belief is present because you are encircled by vortex power.

Bell Rock viewed from Airport Mesa

Some people have dramatic body sensations while working with the energy of Airport. Whether you are aware of your feelings or not, you could have some of these dramatic experiences. Even those quite in tune with their emotions are very moved and surprised here. On one journey, Marcy S., a receptionist, felt as if she were having a heart attack. The energy focused on lessons about self love. She said:

> "I felt incredible guilt for coming to Sedona in the first place. I was having a lot of family problems at the time, and the timing seemed wrong. I felt this awful pain in my chest and arm almost instantly on getting out of my car at Airport Mesa. The pain increased as I was getting closer to what I believe to be the center of the energy. That center, to me, is near the big medicine wheel. I was scared to death. I had no idea what was happening to me. I started going through an array of emotions.
>
> I know Airport helps release these things from home so I started letting the emotions go with each thought I had by filling rocks with my thoughts and letting them fly off the edge of the cliff. I finally concluded that the pain was about my guilt, and my letting the emotions go over the edge was the beginning of opening to loving myself. I know that Airport brings things up that are in the way. Once I saw that, and began working with the energy to release home and all those emotions, I felt better."

Most visitors of the vortexes have stated that they were at a point of major change in their lives. The vortexes acknowledge the need for these changes. Airport helps define that which needs to be addressed, and provides the strength necessary to accept the changes.

The energy of Airport is used for cleansing and releasing all concerns, guilt, angers, and fears that you may be lugging around. Phil G., a college student from Hillsboro, Oregon, remembers "I was able to let go of daily life so I could concentrate on my personal issues at hand." Airport enhances change and release. The awakening comes in the release of the mind so that the body can accept and take in the active, physical, electric energy of Airport.

Cathedral Rock viewed from Airport Mesa

Once you have released home, guilt, and fear, allow yourself to fill with dreams and visions of a better tomorrow. Define your hopes and dreams by writing them in your journal or diary. Listen within to learn how possible these dreams are. Do not limit how you will achieve your goals, only believe that you can. These are two of the gifts of Airport: the physical release of old baggage and the possibility of receiving your dreams. In fact, it will even help you realize how to create those dreams. You need only be open to receiving what Airport Mesa has to offer.

The medicine wheel with friends at Airport Mesa

Questions To Be Answered At Airport Mesa

The following are questions to keep in mind while at Airport Mesa, where one centers around where life is in this moment. Do try to keep in mind that you are within the physical, electric energy of Airport Mesa while you contemplate the following items. Create a connection to the energy through your breathing. Refer to page 178 for more information about breathing. You may receive your answers in symbols, words, etc. Be sure and write your thoughts below.

1. It is useful at Airport to identify, or express why you have come to Sedona. Write below why you have chosen to come to Sedona at this time.

2. Is there any unusual excitement, anxiousness, fear, etc. within you as you are here at Airport Mesa? Describe what you are sensing.

....
....
....
....
....
....

3. What are your concerns at this moment (not to solve the concerns but define them)?

....
....
....
....
....
....
....
....

4. What do you hope will be the outcome of your visit to Sedona?

....
....
....
....
....
....

Issue Releasing Exercise

This exercise helps release that which one no longer wants to carry, through a ceremony of throwing out issues brought from home, such as guilt for spending the money or taking the time, anger at yourself or others, or even fear of what may be wanting to come forward.

As you quiet yourself, note the spiraling energy moving up through the rocks, through your body and into the heavens. Observe the energizing effect that comes about.

Find a stone that will represent your concerns. Begin rhythmically breathing in the vortex energy while you are placing those concerns into the stone by a meditation process, or by concentrating on those things that seem to hinder you from enjoying your experience. Let the stone symbolize those hindrances. Once you feel that your concerns are firmly placed in the stone, energetically toss it over the edge of the vortex. Be careful that no one is below you when you toss your stones!

This exercise represents your release of the issues that you are holding on to. Use as many stones as necessary to feel free of the burdens that followed you to the vortexes. Once you are able to move all burdens, answer the following questions.

1. What did you feel needed to be released?

   ....
   ....
   ....
   ....
   ....
   ....

2. What were your thoughts or feelings while releasing the concerns?

   ....
   ....
   ....
   ....
   ....
   ....

3. Did you receive any visual or mental messages, or symbols while doing this exercise? If so describe them.

   ....
   ....
   ....
   ....
   ....
   ....

4. Did your body experience sensations during or after the completion of the releasing process? Describe what you felt.

....
....
....
....
....
....
....

Releasing concerns over the edge of Airport Mesa

Purpose and Commitment

Airport Mesa is a perfect place to make a commitment to what you want to change in your life, or to looking deeper into yourself. Whatever your desired outcome for the time you spend with the vortexes, you will want to solidify it here. Write below your purpose or intent for your time in Sedona. Once it is written, create a statement of commitment to that purpose.

Purpose:

Commitment:

"The Night Fire"

Chakra Cleansing Meditation

Refer to the chakra diagram on page --- if you do not know where the chakra centers are in your body. You may want to record the meditation so that you can listen and concentrate on the meditation rather than having to read it. Use headphones so as to not disturb others on the vortexes. The following meditation is presented at sunset and therefore utilizes the night sky.

> Put yourself into a peaceful, quiet, meditative state before beginning this meditation.

We are here now at the beautiful place called Airport Mesa. This is the place of the night fire. It is gentle, but it is alive and at this moment you are connecting to the aliveness of this fire. You are here to make friends with this fire because it is a purifying moment. It is a moment that you will release through the fire. This is a place where you are going to see, to feel, to believe. This is the place where you come into aliveness.
(PAUSE)
Let us begin by concentrating on our first chakra, our place of security. Take the color red from the night sky and move it into your first chakra.
(PAUSE)

Take a moment and think about your survival and personal sense of security.
(PAUSE)
To that sense of security, add the color red to your first chakra and let it bathe you with a belief in your own ability to create inner, as well as outer, security. Wear your own inner security and connection to your earth.
(PAUSE)
As you are allowing this acceptance, know that you are safe to believe in yourself because you are capable and unique. Remember, you already have this security and connection. You do not have to manifest it because is already yours. Move the red back out to the sky, filled with the security and connection to earth. See how brilliant it is blended with your color.
(PAUSE)
Feel it...See it...Believe it.
(PAUSE)
Believe that you can be free of any emotions or fears that may be causing imbalance in your life. Let the color orange from the sky connect with your second chakra. Believe that all is safe within you, and that as you connect with the sky in your second chakra through your emotional energy, believe that you can be free of all emotional imbalances. Believe that you can have balance of your emotional self.
(PAUSE)
Put the color orange back out into the sky, watch it go. The sky will light up with this radiant color. It will be orange, bright and beautiful because you are creating it. Believe that you are creating this.
(PAUSE)
Feel it...See it...Believe it.

(PAUSE)
Now let us move into your third chakra. Let the beautiful color of yellow move from the sky into your third chakra. Yellow is the color of the sun, now setting. Let your third chakra connect to the sun; the energy of day, the energy of movement.
(PAUSE)
Release any angers, doubts in your abilities, any belief in a lack you may have, by filling the sky with your yellow. Let the yellow fill the night sky. It is bright and alive because you are allowing it. You are moving your energy into the fire of the sky.
(PAUSE)
Feel it... See it... Believe it...Know that you have created this fire with your third chakra.
(PAUSE)
And all your lower self is purified. You are free.

Let us move into the heart. As you bring the night fire into your heart, it carries the color pink. It is balancing and you are connecting with the night sky in your fourth chakra, your heart.
(PAUSE)
In your heart, you are accepting where you are. You are believing in yourself as to where and who you are. Believe that you love yourself and begin to purify yourself by putting your pink heart, your love energy, back into the fire. Your love is burning in the night fire.
(PAUSE)
Feel it...See it...Believe it.
(PAUSE)
And now let us go to the throat. The place you speak who you are, your fifth chakra. The blue speaks to the fire and draws it into your throat chakra from the sky. Feel it.

And it is purified. See it. See the sky that you are creating as you release the blue. See the sky that you are purifying. Believe it. Because you are allowing, because you are believing, because you are letting yourself be, all is purified.
(PAUSE)
Now let us go to the third eye, your sixth chakra. Bring in the color indigo from the night sky. Your third eye is now gently opening and you know that you can connect into the fire and that the dark blue of knowing is alive. You can feel it, you can see it, you know it. You believe.
(PAUSE)
You are cleansing your third eye through this connection. Know you can. Move the indigo through your third eye into the night fire.
(PAUSE)
You now know that your journey is absolutely possible. Your journey is perfect. You can let go and be free.
(PAUSE)
Feel it...See it...Believe it.
(PAUSE)
And now we go to the crown, your seventh chakra. Move the color purple from the sky through your crown. Allow your spirituality to connect to the sky as it quiets.
(PAUSE)
Move the purple back into the sky and know that you created this sky; that your spiritual self is in that sky.
(PAUSE)
You can see it... You know it... You believe it.
(PAUSE)
You trust yourself. You know. You create your reality. And your reality is this colorful sky. It is beautiful with

the array of colors that you have created. You are now centered and focused. You are ready.
(PAUSE)
Accept your own colorfulness and your ability to create through viewing this beautiful sky. What do you want to create right now?
(PAUSE)
Let your creation be accepted by the colors above you. See it blend and become the colors. Know it is yours.
(PAUSE)
Take a deep breath and take in all your color as you return. Take in the vibration of Airport because this is the place of gentle awakening. Peacefully return to the present filled with the awareness of your own existence as part of this universe.

The medicine wheel at Airport Mesa

Airport Mesa
Personal Observations

Bell Rock

*"This is the place that things mix up
so they can come out straight"*

Bell Rock is the most visible and "energy active" of the vortexes. It is unique, and unmistakable. Bell is an electric vortex; it pulsates with an intense, spiraling energy which draws people to it.

As you approach Bell, you feel something alive and intense. The ground rumbles beneath you. It feels as if there is an underground current constantly stirring things up inside your. The invisible stream charges through you as you begin to walk the trail. You notice that Bell is far away and that it could be a long walk before you touch the full force

of its energy. The sandy trail is lined with rocks and it feels as if you are stepping onto a soft version of the Wizard of Oz's yellow brick road. You feel a sense of adventure or excitement growing much like that which Dorothy must have felt as she began her journey.

You will notice song birds and lizards, but their impression is fleeting because of the energy force of which you have become a part. You are surrounded by juniper, manzanita and scrubbrush, and within minutes, you reach the end of the trail and you see the brilliant red rocks. As you are fully consumed by the charge of Bell, you are exploding with its intensity. You step onto the rocks and the energy starts to erupt inside of you. Looking around, you begin to believe that you may have just walked into the Emerald City, which has turned a vibrant red. A city full of adventure, lessons to learn, and truths to express.

The burst of energy drives you farther up onto the rocks and each step becomes lighter and more animated. Looking out you see the road below you, surprised to realize that you are so far away from your car and only fifteen minutes have passed. Laughing at yourself for believing that this would be such a long hike, you begin to wonder if this is how Bell's energy works. You believe that a task will be time consuming and difficult, but in actuality, when you allow yourself, for example, to be filled with the strength of Bell, life becomes uncomplicated and begins to move steadily. A sense of lightness and adventure is everywhere. Is this how Dorothy felt in the land of Oz?

Stay aware of how you are feeling because electric energy intensifies the space you are in. If you are elated, you will feel more elation. If you are irritated or confused, these feelings become intensified. Be aware of how you feel as you approach Bell. Make adjustments in your thoughts and emotions so that you will be able to flow with Bell in the most beneficial way. Here, action is necessary to move what is being held inside. You are quickly filled with Bell's energy when you arrive and may want to run or dance. You may even want to climb to the top.

    David found, on one of his visits, that as he was driving towards Bell, he was beginning to accelerate his car. The closer he came to Bell, the faster he drove. Soon, he actually heard the screech of his tires as he sped through the curves. He said "Once I parked, I literally ran up Bell. I was so moved by the pull. I ran up Bell, as fast as I was driving my car to Bell! Once I stopped, I saw that I was farther up Bell than I wanted to be. I saw that I had been drawn into the vortex energy before I realized it. I was drawn into the action and movement. From this experience, I learned that climbing the ladder of success (or Bell in this case) may not lead you to your hearts desire (or where you wanted to be). I learned that I needed to stay in the moment and not to rush ahead without being aware of where I am going."

David's experience of being pulled by Bell reminds us of the movie "Close Encounters of the Third Kind." Richard Dreyfuss was pulled to create the mountain, Devils Tower, in Wyoming. Once he created the mountain in his living room, he was compelled to find it. Nothing would stop him from reaching the mountain. Bell holds that kind of pull for some people. If you see Bell in your dreams, or find yourself absentmindedly doodling pictures of bells, you are being called to go and touch Bell Rock. Once there, you will feel as if you are home.

Just as Devil's Tower was a landing spot for space ships, Bell Rock is a landing, as well as a fueling station, for ships. The area between Bell and Courthouse Rock is a portal between space and earth. Ships fly through this area as they surround Bell.

Many people have reported seeing ships in this area and their experiences are chronicled in numerous Sedona books already published, such as "The Mysteries of Sedona" by Tom Dongo. Personally, one evening we saw a ship dart through the sky and suddenly stop. We attempted to communicate by asking the ship to move in specific directions. We requested several different directions and movements and the ship moved in each direction requested. An airplane then flew near the lights and the ship stopped its dance and zoomed away.

Bell is well known for its space connection, but it has many other valuable energies. It is a place of action, movement and cleansing, and because it is fast moving energy, negative issues as well as past life karmas can move very quickly. You may have done things that you wish you had not, but you do not know how to let them go. You may have said or felt things that you wish you had not, but do not know how to free yourself of them. You can move them at Bell. One woman described Bell as "unrelenting, yet safe to release whatever I had been holding." Difficult or frightening issues can move, if you let them.

At Bell, physically connect your body to the rock. In other words, lie or sit on the rocks so as to establish a conscious connection to the energy. Allow the cleansing by simply taking in the energy. To move an issue, you need to recognize it, reexperience it, and finally release it. This is done by holding a picture of what you want to release in your mind's eye and then physically experience it through the energy of Bell. Let yourself be open to understanding why you are holding onto the issue. Do not analyze or question what you receive. Forgive yourself for what you feel or see and allow the energy to flow.

A quiet, inner searching moment

Physical healing is possible here. Bell's energy can move physical, as well as emotional blocks that are manifesting through your health. In changing the old patterns you will free your body of the ailments created by the old patterns. If an unaccustomed pain surfaces acknowledge the pain, ask if there is anything for you to understand, thank it for its message, and release it.

A past life experience that you had forgotten or were not aware of could surface. Acknowledge it. Bless it for showing itself to you. If there is any physical discomfort surrounding this experience, you can easily release it. This is the place of movement. Understand it and then move it.

As a rule of thumb on Bell, stay focused. It is easy to drift and not pay attention to what you are doing. It is best to have an idea of what you would like to work on, and to have a plan so as to help the focus. Be present with the energy, not the information that is being given to you, or you will lose touch with the energy flow. Write down the information and then let it go. Information comes fast and flits away, so you must be present in the moment to get that which is here for you.

Energy releases on Bell can be very intense. We have watched intense expressions of emotion from many people while on Bell. In comparison, Airport is very gentle and mild, and issues surface more gracefully. Bell has been likened to a microwave oven, while Airport is an outdoor barbecue. Sometimes we need to micro things; especially those which are already understood, but that we just cannot seem to physically let go. Other issues need a combination of answers and energies before they are ready to be released.

Tara, a massage therapist, experienced Bell Rock as a place of rebirth. She said:

"It was like coming home. I had no control and needed to totally let go and be with it. I needed to totally surrender to the process. It was a bit scary and embarrassing at first, but soon I felt "old" or even primal. This helped me reconnect in a way to my ancient knowingness. I think this happened because I was open to any and all possibilities while here. It was like the center of the earth opened up and my own Goddess self emerged."

You may potentially, after your first visit to Bell, experience some fear or trepidation about returning. This feeling passes. The first visit may have surprised you with emotional explosions. However, the return visit will be to a familiar place and you will be emotionally prepared for Bell to bring forth almost anything.

Bell is an exhilarating and eye opening experience. One man, on his second visit, saw Bell as steady with a swift pace. "It is a place where I could face my fears. It is a place where you **earn** peace. It can be intimidating. I found myself channeling for the second time here. It was a different style of writing from before." Each person is different and walks life in different ways. Bell may or may not attract you. Either way, you will still receive some wonderful releases and energy movements by just being in Bell's energy.

One last note, do not come to Bell in the evening, not only because of the many space brothers and unknown energies, but also because of the shadows that begin to fall at dusk. The energy changes dramatically as the sun sets. Through our own naivete, and innocence, we have experienced the drastic changes in the energy of Bell as the sun begins to set. It becomes very uncomfortable and uninviting. It seemed to take on a "cold" energy. Your perception of time and space will be different and you could become disoriented when you try to leave. There are also the physical dangers of trying to get off the rocks as shadows are falling. The sun sets much faster than one suspects and if you are not prepared and experienced in night hiking, you could easily fall off the crags.

Questions To Be Answered At Bell Rock

Bell Rock is the place that vibrates with space/physical energy. One is able to release and cleanse here. Keep the following questions in mind while on Bell Rock. Be sure to write your thoughts below.

1. Bell represents a vortex energy of movement. Describe any changes you may experience while on Bell.

   ....
   ....
   ....
   ....
   ....
   ....
   ....
   ....

2. How do these changes affect you?

   ....
   ....
   ....
   ....
   ....
   ....
   ....

3. What beliefs do you have about change?

4. Express up to four things you would like to change in your life.

Connecting with the Indents

Look for an indent in the rocks to lie in as you do these exercises. The energy of Bell comes up through these indents. An indent, with an example of how to lie in it is pictured below. As you lie in these spots, you will be a part of Bell's energy flow.

Do keep breathing. It moves the energy. You may want to refer to page 178 concerning Proper Breathing. When working with vortex energy it is important to continually breathe in a deep and rhythmic manner, creating a circular motion. The vortex energy is in the rocks around you as well as in the air. When you breathe you take it in.

A view of the land from Bell Rock

Directions for the Indents Exercise

Allow Bell's energy to bring forward any blocks that are prominent for you, or you may establish a specific focus. For example focus on the blocks to receiving the four things that you would like to change in your life. Look for any blocks to change, joy, work, family, relationships, security, anger, fears, physical pains or past life influences.

If you use a specific focus, determine what it will be before you begin your connection with the energy. Once you connect with the energy, allow yourself to accept whatever is showing and keep it moving through your breathing. Do not forget the importance of breathing with the vortexes. The more conscious you are, the more you will take in the vibration, which will balance your body with the energy.

The indents are grooves, often oval in shape in the rocks. The energy comes up through the dip in the indent. This is healing energy and it has been said that crystals are under the rocks in these spaces.

There are many ways to lie in the indents so as to create a connection with Bell. For example:

1. Lie on your back in the indent, with your head to Bell for at least five minutes. Turn over and lay on your stomach for another five minutes. Different things will surface and be released when laying on your stomach as opposed to your back. While connected with Bell you will see and feel things move in your body. Allow whatever is coming forward to keep moving. Accept what you see or feel and let it go. Keep breathing!

2. Repeat the above example with your feet towards Bell. Do what feels right for you.

For more ideas on how to work with the indents, read "Working with your Chakras - Indent Exercise Options" on the following page.

A group of friends working together on Bell Rock

Working with your Chakras Indent Exercise Options

These options can help you connect with Bell's energy as you walk with the indents. Once in connection with the energy, establish a focus and allow whatever is showing to be released. If you want more information about chakras, refer to page 179.

1. Lay on the rocks and let yourself feel the energy of the vortex come forward. Lay on your stomach and feel your chakras open up as the energy of Bell moves up through the rocks.

2. Sit on the ground and with your feet touching the ground, visualize your feet chakras opening. Move the energy up through the feet and then out each chakra point. Have the color of each chakra flow out each center and then up through your crown. Keep this continuously moving up, and through, and out... up and, through, and out... Let the colors of each chakra blend together in front of you as you move up into and through each chakra.

3. Lay on your back with your feet towards Bell. Move the energy in through your feet, up through the backside and out the front chakras. This is a good exercise in that it removes unwanted energy stuck in the chakras that could stop the energy flow. It creates a complete cleansing.

4. For any of the indent exercises you could use chakra or healing stones. You can place crystals at the top and bottom of your person and allow the stones to aid the movement of the energy.

5. As you bring the energy of Bell into each chakra point, ask that chakra center what it is holding onto that it would like to release. Ask why it has been holding it so that you will have an understanding of the situation. Once you understand, let it move through the chakra center into the air. Use the color of that chakra to assist you. Once the situation is moved, fill the chakra center with white light. Move to the next chakra point and repeat the exercise.

The view from Bell Rock

Meditation of Light

You may want to record this meditation so that you can concentrate on it while at Bell. Use headphones when doing this meditations so as to not interrupt other visitors. Do this meditation while laying in an indent, on your back with your head towards Bell. Combine it with one of the Indent Exercises. They will flow together beautifully. Begin with the meditation so that you will be relaxed and receptive to Bell's energy. Once complete with the meditation, flow into the Indent Exercise.

Read through the directions for the Indent Exercise before beginning the meditation so you will be able to continue the flow without interruption. It is best to be barefoot when working with these exercises. The longer you are barefoot, the more you will take in the vibration.

Meditation of Light

*Put yourself in a peaceful meditative state
before beginning the meditation.*

Visualize the earth radiating a beautiful white light, with the light touching every person, every animal, every plant, the water, the sky, the buildings, everything. See everything upon the earth being filled with this white light.
(PAUSE)

See every person and thing being cleansed with the light. It is moving up through them and out to the heavens, up through the atmosphere, cleansing the atmosphere and clouds of any radiation or negativity.
(PAUSE)
Keep allowing the circulation of white light.
(PAUSE)
Visualize a healing vibration moving into your earth. See the earth accepting it.
(PAUSE)
See this to be more than enough energy for the earth to bring it back, up and out, and that it circulates through every person, plant, animal and thing on the earth.
(PAUSE)
Let yourself now be a part of this circle of healing light. See yourself fill up and overflow with the light.
(PAUSE)
Once you feel totally filled, begin concentrating on a connection with Bell. Let your light now start to flow up to Bell and then return from under the rocks and into you. Feel the circle of energy from Bell, through you and back to Bell.

As soon as you are complete with the above meditation roll over and continue allowing the flow of energy from the rocks through you to Bell. Keep the circle moving. Allow whatever is surfacing to be released. Keep breathing in the energy!

Flow into any of the Indent Exercises you have chosen.

Personal Observations
While at Bell Rock

Cathedral Rock

The Home of Inner Peace

Lemuria and the Dolphins

The essence of Lemuria permeates the Sedona area, specifically Cathedral Rock and many people have established intense connections with dolphins while here. Perhaps the connection is easier in this particular place because it holds that quieter, intuitive, knowing energy that matches the Lemurian essence.

The Lemurians were a highly evolved race of people that believed in fairness and living a spiritual life. They were intuitive and worked a great deal with third eye energy. They were a race of healers who shared their knowledge and ability with each other. They knew that all creatures and things of nature were special and had a purpose that was to be shared.

They were aware of the knowledge that dolphins carry and created a working relationship with them. Many people have felt, and inwardly sensed dolphins while at Cathedral as well as at other vortex spots. One journey friend said "I had glimpses of dolphins in my arms and felt like I was physically touched on my shoulder." Another friend, Lucy P., a Mari-EL practitioner, from Gresham, Oregon, received the touch of the dolphins at Bell Rock. She remembers:

"In October of 1991, the first tinme I came to Sedona I did not know anything about Lemuria or the dolphins. I went to Bell Rock and began to meditate. Dolphins appeared to the right, then to the left of my inner vision. One became brave and touched me on both sides of my neck whispering a message that was mysteriously transmitted. Over the next year, this message unfolded exactly as predicted by the dolphin."

There are many scientific experts that agree that there was a continent, or at least a large land mass in the Pacific Ocean that is no longer visible except for a few islands that could be mountain tops. There are also many books written, from the scientific to the psychic, that have touched on the possibility of Lemuria. Although there are volumes now in print discussing the touch of Lemuria and dolphins in this area, it can not be proven. So, instead of debating on the validity, play with the possibility. Quiet yourself and see if you can envision the Lemurians living here and bonding with the dolphins.

Back O'Beyond

The approach to Cathedral Rock takes you into the quiet as you turn onto Back O'Beyond Road. It is a winding, gravel road that forces you to enter the silence slowly. Through the silence, you feel the serenity that seems to envelop this area. As you look at the horizon, you see a stunning structure that seems immense, yet delicate and feminine. The red rocks form several statuesque columns, pinnacles of beauty. These give the appearance of a Cathedral or temple and awaken a sense of devotion and willingness to reach into the heart. Speech becomes difficult in this reverent, heavenly scene, and the sense of devotion occurs almost as a reflex to the beauty.

Continuing down the dusty road, each turn offers a view of Cathedral Rock, each grander and larger than before, which strengthens your desire to enter the silence and receive the gifts Cathedral offers. You soon reach the parking area and Cathedral lies ahead of you, drawing you gently into her peace. Once out of your car, you drop into a dry creek bed and then, come upon a trail that invites you to respond to her call.

The energy of Cathedral, on the surface, feels very peaceful and serene. It is, but it is also much more than that. Because it is magnetic in nature, it opens within us our intuitive, feeling, feminine, spiritual and loving side. Our deeper, softer side surfaces and we accept our creative abilities and knowingness. We also open up to past lives, forgotten memories and hidden potentials. Sue K., a salesperson from Oak Harbor, Washington, had just such an experience. She remembers:

"Things came to me about my past as well as my childhood at Cathedral. Things about my family came up and I realized how everyone was pitted against each other. I saw the reality about my dad and how he was not really there for me. He did not really support me like I had pretended he had. Reality struck hard. My rose colored glasses were taken off and I saw things as they were. Another veil was lifted. Cathedral helped that to happen for me."

We are willing to search our inner selves because the nurturing energy helps us know it will be safe. Phillip remembers "I felt like I was being cradled in someone's arms." These arms are powerful in what they can show us about ourselves. Another visitor recognized that "she talks to me as if she knows me. I received wonderful messages here." We let our true self come forward in this sensitive, mysterious place.

This particular area of Cathedral Rock works strongly with the pinnacles, the spires of rock that reach into the heavens. They are the energy centers of this side of the vortex and through connecting with them you connect with your needs. The energy moves up the pinnacles and then down to spots on the ground, to which you will feel the energy come through your head and out your feet. Become part of the flow and connect through your energy to the fullness of this magnetic pulse.

To address your needs, begin with a commitment to be open to receiving that which is right for you at this time. Release preconceived ideas about yourself and let the unique, feeling, knowing part of you emerge. Ask about your emotional needs and move into a state of receptivity so that the pinnacles and Cathedral energy can connect with you.

The pinnacles of Cathedral Rock

Allow yourself to feel. Say a prayer of affirmation, such as "I allow feeling to be present. I accept what is. I will take no less." If the intention is to be quiet and receive, the energy will support it. Needs are understood and accepted here. A belief that you can fulfill those needs strengthens you to search even while in a vulnerable state. Inner knowing can shift into living even if we do not completely understand. Trust that you are moving in the right direction for you. At Cathedral, simply allow yourself to accepted and be held. Once you allow yourself to accept the support, you will find beauty in the knowledge received. By the time you leave this temple, you will have a volume of answers.

Quiet time on Cathedral Rock

The pinnacles use symbols as a method of communication with those who are connected to them. Our imagination awakens and symbols become very vivid. Accept the symbols as they are presented. Do not analyze, but rather take the symbols in and hold them. Let your inner knowing embrace them and receive their message.

Joe S., from Seattle, Washington wanted to make peace with the loneliness in his life on one visit to Cathedral. While in connection with the pinnacles, he had the following experience:

"I saw a winged horse, which seemed to give me a great deal of stability. I was feeling intense loneliness that went away when I had the support of the horse. The horse kept getting bigger, no matter what part of my block was showing. Even when the fear of the moment showed, I noticed the horse was already bigger than it. This was very significant to me. I now know I have support for my loneliness. I could even feel the horse's coat and how powerful it was. I still carry it with me."

The power of the pinnacles also expresses itself through soft whispers that draw you into their circle of energy. You awaken to knowledge about yourself because this energy by-passes logic and moves you into feeling. You could experience soft tears here because you allow yourself be a part of an inner journey that reaches into the depths of self love. From his willingness to be supported, Joe S. realized that he could be loved and open to receiving by his willingness to be vulnerable.

He also felt as if he were coming home while here. He stated that "It was an intense feeling like "mom." I couldn't stop crying. The energy was graceful and powerful, yet soft. It was like a part of me. I did not want to leave."

You are vulnerable and sensitive, and issues tend to take on new meaning when in connection with Cathedral energy. People have been known to be sensitive to sound, words and the energy of others while here. They are more aware of animals and the natural surroundings. Colors appear more vivid because of these sensitivities. Connection with friends while in this energy will be fragile. This vulnerable state is because each in a self-evaluating, inner journey state. What comes for you may not be understood by your friends because they are deep in their own search. Your personal sensitivities may overshadow conversations and cause you to hear or feel the words of others wrong. Therefore, allow yourself, and your friends, personal time at Cathedral. Two to four hours of silence is optimum. Respect each other's space and needs. Spend the time without conversation. This holds for the walk off Cathedral as well. Let simple, heartfelt conversation begin as you retrace your steps on the gravel road that leads back to everyday living.

Questions to be Answered at Cathedral Rock
(Back O'Beyond)

The following are questions to keep in mind while at Cathedral, where one goes inside and begins to listen. Relax and let yourself explore your answers. Be sure and write your thoughts below.

1. What are your emotional needs?

   ....
   ....
   ....
   ....

2. When you ask to have your emotional needs met, what sensitivities (feelings) do you experience?

   ....
   ....
   ....
   ....

3. Do you trust that your emotional needs will be met? Why or why not?

   ....
   ....
   ....
   ....

4. What fears become manifest when you look at your emotional needs?

....
....
....
....

5. What fears stand in the way of believing that your emotional needs will be met?

....
....
....
....

6. What conclusions do you draw about your fears about your emotional needs?

....
....
....
....
....

Now that you are aware of your fears you can allow yourself to open to new possibilities. This inner peace comes from the acceptance of the unknown.

7. How do you access your inner knowledge? (Some methods of accessing this knowledge could be through pictures, stories, symbols, colors, sound, coincidences and inner guidance.)

8. What happens when you allow yourself to trust this information without specifically understanding if it fits or what it means?

9. What conclusions have you drawn about yourself in regards to fear and trust?

Preparation To The Pinnacle Exercise

You may stay in one spot while working with the pinnacles or you may want to move around. Whatever you need to do is fine. Each pinnacle may require different energy spots on the ground as well as different ways of working with it.

Do not worry if you do not have enough time to find all of the issues while here. Take the time to truly search the ones you feel are most important. While working with the pinnacles, notes must be taken. Nothing will stay in your head. By the time you move on to the next phase, you may potentially lose everything already presented.

Pinnacle Exercise

1. Draw and number the pinnacles as you see them.

2. Find your power spot on the ground by allowing yourself to be guided inspirationally or intuitively to a spot where you can meditate.

3. Feel the vortex energy move from the pinnacles into and through the top of your head, down and out the bottoms of your feet, into the earth and back to the pinnacles. This circle of energy will continue as you maintain an awareness of your breathing.

4. Begin meditating on the pinnacle that is calling to you and ask "What may I receive regarding my emotional needs?" Next ask "What lessons or issues are part of this?" And then wait. The information could come in symbols, pictures, stories, words, colors, past life information or childhood experiences.

5. Record what you receive from the pinnacles on the page titled: "Pinnacle Information Received"

Drawing of the Pinnacles

Pinnacle Information Received

Pinnacle # _____ presented the following information.

....
....
....
....
....
....

Pinnacle # _____ presented the following information.

....
....
....
....
....
....

Pinnacle # _____ presented the following information.

....
....
....
....
....
....

Pinnacle # _____ presented the following information.

Pinnacle # _____ presented the following information.

Pinnacle # _____ presented the following information.

Pinnacle # _____ presented the following information.

_____
_____
_____
_____
_____
_____
_____

Pinnacle # _____ presented the following information.

_____
_____
_____
_____
_____
_____
_____

Pinnacle # _____ presented the following information.

_____
_____
_____
_____
_____
_____
_____

Reclaiming Your Essence

You will journey to Lemuria while swimming with the dolphins. You will touch the vibration of your essence and become one, again, with all that you have been. Find a spot that is comfortable. The dolphins are here and ready to welcome you. When you connect with them you will see their beauty. You may want to talk this meditation into a tape recorder so that you can concentrate on the exercise. Use headphones while listening to the meditation so as to not disturb others on the vortex.

Begin to breath in this land of Lemuria. Hold inside of you the energy of Lemuria, the energy of now, and know that all time is now. Release time and move into inner knowing. You will be free to be yourself. Breath in Lemuria. Breath in the freedom of expression and move into yourself. Feel the flow of life through your body. Feel it move with you.
(PAUSE)
Connect with the flow of life. Know that, in this moment, all moments are yours, all that has been so perfect about you is here, with you. Begin to relax and release the body and become your soul self, your essence. Become who you have been through all time, let all be

now, and be your essence, be your light. In your oneness you can feel the essence of self and through this essence look around and see that all of life is right now.
(PAUSE)
Look around and see the beautiful flowers, and blue, turquoise blue water in front of you. It is clear and you can see all the way to the bottom of the waters. It invites you to enter the water and swim.
(PAUSE)
As you are swimming these waters you see the fish. Some are bright yellows and greens while others are all colors of the rainbow. Some fish are very tiny and some are very large. You can see their aliveness. You see their essence. You see that they are perfect as they are.
(PAUSE)
As you move deeper into this ocean, you see that the flowers that were above the water are also below the water, and that they are bright reds and yellows, and they vibrate. You can actually feel them vibrating through the turquoise water. One flower is sending sound to you. It is speaking to you. Be one with it and listen to the flower. What piece of wisdom does this flower give you?
(PAUSE)
Wrap yourself in the flower's essence. Blend into the flower now. Be one with it. Take its color into your essence.
(PAUSE)
Recognize the color of the flower and become that color within yourself.
(PAUSE)
You are reclaiming your piece of the plant kingdom. The color that you have become is your plant essence color.

When you want to connect with the plant kingdom, this is the color that you create to become one with it. Hold it well in your essence.
(PAUSE)
Thank the flower for its gift. Separate now, holding the essence of the plant kingdom, but releasing the flower to be its own beauty again.
(PAUSE)
And now, keep moving through the water, through this beautiful turquoise water. You come upon the rock and the sand of the bottom of the ocean. It is a beautiful color, this rock, this sand. Touch the sand.
(PAUSE)
Through your essence, reach into the color of the sand. The beautiful browns and yellows and greens and oranges and blues and reds, all colors are in the sand. Look closely, see the colors.
(PAUSE)
The colors are crystal clear and you can see through them. They are as clear as light as you look. Touch them. Watch your hands, your essence becomes light and clear as you hold the color.
(PAUSE)
Blend into that sand, into that rock. Become one with it.
(PAUSE)
Know that you are the earth, you are the sands of time, you are the sands of light.
(PAUSE)
Hold it in your essence. It is yours. Feel it, become one. Your essence contains the earth. You hold the mineral kingdom.
(PAUSE)
Take it in, become one, and ask the sand what may I

remember that I have always known from you?
(PAUSE)
Be one with the mineral kingdom. Know that it is yours. The earth holds life and you are one with it. Hold it well. Know the essence of this earth, of these minerals, of this land. Remember that you have always known this knowledge, it is ancient with you. It is who you are. The sand and the earth and the rock are willing to give it to you, to reawaken it within you.
(PAUSE)
Release the earth, release the sand, holding the essence within you. Hold the knowledge, but let the earth now be its light, be its own clarity within itself. Within you, hold the earth wisdom. It is yours.
(PAUSE)
Continue moving your spirit, your essence through the water where you will be welcomed by the dolphins. You see the pod in front of you as you move through a beautiful opening. They wait for you. They greet you.
(PAUSE)
Connect with the dolphin that is coming towards you. Become one with that dolphin, now, for this dolphin is the self of long ago. It is who you have been, it is who you are. This dolphin is your essence now. Become one, blend with it.
(PAUSE)
Recognize that it holds your balance, be it your male side, be it your female side. This dolphin holds the balance for you. It holds the oneness. Blend with that part of yourself. See your essence become one with the other part of yourself that this dolphin holds.
(PAUSE)
Begin to move, move with the dolphin through the water.

Feel the essence of the water, feel the freedom of the movement, feel the self flowing, and be one with the water through the dolphin, through your other half.
(PAUSE)
Move with it, blend and flow.
(PAUSE)
And this half of you moves you through the water until you come, again, to the shore. But it is a new shore. It is a shore you have not walked for a long, long time. Be one with your dolphin as you look at the shore.
(PAUSE)
The dolphin is inviting you to receive your other half. The message of the dolphin is to take your other half with you and to begin to walk on to the shore.
(PAUSE)
Release the dolphin, but hold onto your other half. Become one, now, with your other half. Know that you are your wholeness. Your male and female are blending. You are in oneness with yourself.
(PAUSE)
Walk from the water onto the shore. You might feel different, you might even look different. You are walking what was perfection for you, what is perfection for you, what is the connection of self to all time.
(PAUSE)
Look at the shore, look at the land. How does it appear to you? How does it look?
(PAUSE)
Go, now, where you need to go. You are in the land of Lemuria. You are in the land of old. You are in the land of right now.
(PAUSE)
In quiet, go where you are guided by your new blend of

self, not by just one part of you, but by your whole self, walk the now, walk the past and receive the messages that are here for you.
(PAUSE)
You are in a perfect place. Look for what can guide you forever.
(PAUSE)
In your journey, there will be something that you have always desired, and it will be there for you to reconnect with, to accept back into your essence in a conscious way. Look for it now, it is in front of you.
(PAUSE)
This is who you are. This is what you walk. This is what you will create, again, because you already know it. You are only now rediscovering it.
(PAUSE)
Take it into your essence. Take this desire that you have found, into that wholeness of self. Breath it in, take it in, it is yours. It is who you are. It is what you can walk. It is what you are. It is from the land of old and it is now remembered.
(PAUSE)
Walk back to the shore with it. Move into the water. Your dolphin waits. But you do not blend this time. Share the ride with the dolphin, because you have the gift. You have the gift of old.
(PAUSE)
You have the gift of the emotion. You have the gift of your wholeness. You have the gift of the earth.
(PAUSE)
See the mineral kingdom, the sand, again, as you move back. Do not connect, you already have it.
(PAUSE)

its essence. Keep moving. You already have all the pieces you need.
(PAUSE)
Return to the shores of now and rest. Look again out into the turquoise waters and just take a moment to understand and accept what you have gathered.
(PAUSE)
The dolphins send their blessings, and they are moving into the water again, until next time.
(PAUSE)
Feel your wholeness. Remember your knowledge, for your purpose is to walk that knowledge now. You only need to create it in earthly steps. It is in you. The vision, the desire, it walks in you.
(PAUSE)
Take a deep breath, and in that breath you accept all that you have known. You are free to be who you are. Bless Lemuria for returning these pieces to you. Begin to open your eyes to the Lemuria of now. This is your home now. This is the beautiful place you have chosen to live now. But you can walk what you have always been, and it is beautiful.

Snow on Cathedral Rock

Personal Observations
Around the Pinnacles

Red Rock Crossing

Another approach to Cathedral Rock begins in a beautiful park named Red Rock Crossing. Newly improved, the park offers numerous parking spaces, picnic tables, barbecues, restrooms and a soft, sandy trail that cushions your feet as you walk.

The trail meanders along Oak Creek and gifts those listening with a medley of sounds: gurgling water, the chirping of birds, the whispering wind rustling through the trees, the laughter and screeches of children and adults alike, that have been enticed into the cool, healing waters of Oak Creek. It seems impossible to keep your shoes on once you have been drawn into the touch of Cathedral's energy.

The most widely photographed spot in Arizona

The trail also gifts those looking with the most breathtaking and picturesque view of Cathedral Rock possible. It rises mysteriously in the background of Oak Creek. In its majesty, this sacred vortex graces the waters with its magnetic healing energy, which we call the "Healing Waters of Cathedral." If you find yourself here, bathe in the waters and let your physical and emotional concerns dissolve into the water. Let your worries drift away and develop a connection to inner harmony. In this receptive state the healing begins.

Oak Creek at Red Rock Crossing

One visitor stated, with a peaceful expression on her face "The waters were so calm and serene, I couldn't move. I believed I had found heaven on earth. I had no desire to go anywhere or do anything. I was in a state of personal and spiritual balance."

You gracefully become a part of the balancing force that is so powerful on this side of Cathedral Rock. The strength of balance is offered to each, in whatever direction that is necessary. You may need balance in partnerships, emotions, or your home life. You may need a balancing of your male and female sides, between work and home, between your spiritual and physical lives, between your self needs with the needs of others. Whatever is out of balance comes to the surface and gives you the opportunity to accept that balance into your life. You see and feel ways that the balances can be possible. You accept the possibilities and begin wearing them like a new set of clothes. They feel good, although different because they are new. This healing is often very subtle and may not even be noticed consciously. You will need to be alert to your feelings, and even to conversations while in these waters so as to notice how they are presenting this balancing energy.

You may stay in the healing waters or continue on to the different levels of Cathedral. To reach the base you must cross the creek and follow another sandy trail on the opposite side of the creek. On this side of Cathedral, the power is highly concentrated around the green rock mass that is located near the center, and at the base of Cathedral. It is directly under the spires that have been called the Male/Female spires. Although the vortex energy is very prominent in this spot, the vortex power blankets the entire area.

The elusiveness of Cathedral presents itself as you begin the journey into the vortex power. The magnetic pull puts you into a state of inner bliss. This creates a bit of a challenge as you are making your ascent up this side of Cathedral. "I actually didn't want to go up the face of Cathedral because I could feel the risk of going into something unknown" said one woman as she approached the trail making its way up Cathedral.

The trail is steep and difficult if you go straight up. Instead, angle your way up, taking mental pictures of the terrain and where you want to head. Be prepared to make frequent stops because it is a strenuous climb.

Remember, the trail matches the energy of Cathedral and can be just as elusive as Cathedral itself. There are many areas of wash-off that give the illusion of being a trail. You can get very confused if you follow the wash-offs as opposed to the actual trail. Therefore, be observant and use landmarks as guideposts for the way up, and especially for the journey down.

One of the faces of Cathedral Rock

Once you have reached your desired destination, which is anywhere you feel drawn to stop and connect with the energy, take a few minutes to enjoy the incredible view. Some have described this area as primitive or untouched by man. "It seems to be unpolluted by human energy," stated a hiker one day. He continued "The air is crisp, clear and pulsates with a primitive, mysterious, yet peaceful feel." Peace permeates the entire area and the inner self begins to blend with this peace. A feeling of total self acceptance will come over you.

The same seeker that did not want to leave the waters of Oak Creek below felt the same sense of peace and balance as she did in the waters. Once she chose to explore this face of Cathedral, she was surprised to feel the similarities of the energies. "I again experienced no future, no past. I was centered into where I needed to be," she stated. Because balance is the strength of this side, you will find yourself beginning to examine unresolved insecurities, or needs, in your life. A very prominent experience on this side is the awakening of the physical self to the deepening of partnerships from whatever level they are at. This happens because the energy of love saturates this area and one feels love become manifest. This side of Cathedral Rock puts <u>you</u> first and helps you see and feel your own importance. Through this you can explore your personal relationships.

Those sharing a healthy, personal connection with someone feel that wonderful bond and make a deeper commitment to that person. Dan remembers:

"It was such a joy to discover this side of Cathedral again. My wife and I had previously camped here but had found it

from the Verde Valley Road. I remembered the full moon, brilliant stars and my first introduction to vortex energy. It was nice to discover this same spot with her four years later. I felt a strong connection to the memories, but also to what we have physically as well as emotionally built since that first camping trip. I believe that first visit here was like a launching pad to what we have now."

Partners allow themselves to be more vulnerable, which allows that deepening, which develops through being truthful about your relationship. You become more aware of what is real and balanced, as well as what needs your attention and honesty. The self love focus of the vortex energy enhances this truthfulness and willingness to investigate all sides of a relationship.

Those in an unhealthy relationship see clearly the need to change things in order to have the love they need. They see very clearly that which is not flowing properly in the relationship. The pains of lost partnerships can show, so that with the vortex energy, you can come to a peaceful balance with them. Losses long ago forgotten may even surface, if they are not resolved in a way that is in balance for you. The essence of self love that engulfs this area becomes stronger than fears of being alone or unloved, and you put yourself first when determining your love needs.

Those not in relationships, yet desire to be, are able to make a connection within themselves so as to allow for that in the future. A knowingness of the loss of touch is felt by many who are not sharing an emotional or physical connection with someone. One young woman emphasized how this area caused her to face herself and the old pains that she would never have a relationship. "I released it by being truthful with myself." This emptiness finds peace and a new commitment so that a partnership can emerge because of first, the vortex focus on self love and then, the acceptance of one's present circumstances. Cathedral helps you know that things now are perfect and necessary for the next step. This knowingness is that which brings peace and then the movement into new adventures.

Partnerships do not stop with just your personal relationships. It also includes the relationships we have with family, work associates, friends, neighbors and all people with whom we come in contact. We see and feel what kind of partner we are to others. How do we create connection, as well as how do we deepen any connection? How vulnerable are we willing to be so as to find love and to accept it into our daily lives? Using self love as the guiding force, we will search honestly within ourselves and establish truthful connections that keep the self, as well as others, honored and recognized.

Once complete with your inner search into self love, it will be time to begin your descent, which can be more challenging than the journey up. You will have spent time in this vortex power and inner things are churning. You will be more tired than when you began the journey, potentially because of the heat and the physical energy used in the climb up Cathedral. Take some time to recollect your energy before beginning your descent. Drink plenty of water or juice and eat some fruit or trail mix to help revitalize you. Disconnect from any meditative state you may have been in. Bring your mind back to the active, alert mode and find the landmarks you established on the way up.

When ready, begin your descent. Think! Be patient and aware of Cathedral's illusive trails. One novice climber to this side saw how treacherous it was to come down when she lost the trail, as well as her footing, and slid straight down twenty feet. Fortunately a flat, loose rock became a toboggan and transported her to safer ground. One can use the gully which is directly in front of the center spires (the male/female spires) as an overall guidepost to walk near. So, walk in balance, be in peace and be careful.

Questions to be Answered at Cathedral Rock
(Red Rock Crossing)

Find a peaceful, quiet spot in the waters of Oak Creek. Once in connection with the water, answer the following questions. Write your thoughts below.

1. What areas of your emotions and physical wellbeing are out of balance?

   ....
   ....
   ....
   ....

2. What physical and emotional pains are preventing you from connecting to inner harmony?

   ....
   ....
   ....
   ....

3. Are there any other blocks surfacing that prevent you from connecting to inner harmony?

   ....
   ....
   ....
   ....

Cleansing in the Waters of Cathedral

1. Find a leaf that will represent the blocks to your inner harmony that you have discovered.

2. Breathe rhythmically and open to the healing energy of Cathedral waters. Let anything held inside be dissolved into the leaf.

3. Release the leaf into the water and feel your body become free of the blocks.

Describe how it felt to release the blocks.

....
....
....
....
....
....
....
....
....
....
....
....
....
....

Balancing with Relationships

The following questions can be answered at the waters, or you can cross the creek and connect with Cathedral at the base, or move up the front towards the center spires. This entire area holds the energy of balance. Relax into a quiet, receptive state before answering the questions.

1. What regarding relationships is asking to be brought into balance?

   ....
   ....
   ....
   ....

2. Describe a relationship that honors your needs and allows you to feel at peace and in personal balance.

   ....
   ....
   ....
   ....

3. Within relationships, what qualities about yourself do you appreciate?

   ....
   ....
   ....
   ....

Understanding Relationships

With an understanding of what relationships mean to you, it is time to ask Cathedral to show you the areas in your life, regarding relationships, that are not in balance. Let the information come in words, symbols, pictures, stories, ideas, etc.

I have received the following information regarding relationships that are not in harmony:

_____
_____
_____
_____
_____
_____
_____
_____
_____

I have drawn the following conclusions regarding myself and the relationships in my life:

_____
_____
_____
_____
_____
_____
_____
_____

Swimming with the Dolphins

This meditation is best experienced at the healing waters with your feet immersed in its loving touch. *This meditation is a fun, joyful way to connect with Cathedral Rock and the dolphin energy that seems to be present.* You may want to talk this meditation into a tape recorder so you can concentrate better on the exercise. Use headphones when listening to the tape so as not to disturb anyone on the vortex.

Let yourself relax and move into the quiet of this place. Listen to the silence and the peace that silence brings.
(PAUSE)
Through the quiet, feel the energy of the water. Let yourself become one with the water. It feels as soft as the clouds in the sky. The water goes deep within you.

(PAUSE)
You are now in the ocean. Let yourself be a part of the ocean. You can swim in this ocean. Allow yourself to become clean through the water. Let yourself swim cleansed, peaceful and free.
(PAUSE)
Feel the peace of swimming so freely. You do not need to breathe because you are one with the water. You are in perfect order.
(PAUSE)
As you are swimming and reaching into the water, feel the cleansing. Let yourself swim now and go deep into the water. Let the cleansing continue.
(PAUSE)
As you are swimming, go deep, deeper into the unknown that is so peaceful. It is so free now to just be.
(PAUSE)
As you now swim, you are greeted by the dolphins. They find you, and their eyes are so gentle, so kind. They come and one in particular comes and talks to you now. Look at your dolphin. Let your dolphin share the moment.
(PAUSE)
Your dolphin is inviting you to climb upon his back and share the ride. You are not too heavy for him. You are perfect because you will hold the dolphin with your arms, with your legs and he can feel your love. Hold your dolphin and let him carry you now and carry you into the peaceful valley of water. Your dolphin is talking, listen...
(PAUSE)
Ask your dolphin for the gift of inner harmony. It is a gift that he has and he is willing to share with you. As you hold your dolphin, you can feel the wonderful, loving

energy that he shares with you. Connect with the energy of inner harmony now.
(PAUSE)
You are ready to give your dolphin what you do not want to carry any longer.
(PAUSE)
In your love, let your dolphin receive your physical or emotional pains. He will swim with them and help you free yourself.
(PAUSE)
You and your dolphin are going into the underwater castles. Look at the piers and pinnacles underneath the water. Swim through them. Enjoy them.
(PAUSE)
This is where the dolphins play. You are free. Your suffering is gone. They have let you go into their land of play. And the pinnacles under the water are so beautiful and so bright in color. And you now play. Perhaps you will want to swim alongside your dolphin. That is okay, you can keep up with him. He is willing to keep the pace you are comfortable with.
(PAUSE)
Ask your dolphin for a personal truth about you. A piece that you can always carry with you and hold to you whenever you are afraid or unsure of yourself.
(PAUSE)
Let your dolphin bring you back to this place now. Back to today. You will remember every part of your journey. Take a deep breath and you will be back into your present journey.

Relax and enjoy the wonderful feeling of Cathedral waters. Write your experience in your journal or diary.

Personal Observations
Cathedral Rock

Boynton Canyon

"Let past lives, forgotten memories and intuitive experiences unfold."

As you approach Boynton Canyon, you begin to feel the peacefulness created by the electro-magnetic vortex energy of this area. This energy is a blend of physical, active energy, with inner, intuitive energy, and is enhanced by the mystique this canyon holds. The vortex energy radiates through the entire area. It abounds and seems to exude from the ground as well as from the rocks and trees. The fullness of the energy adds to the beauty of the landscape which is immense, full and inspiring. You can walk Boynton any time of the day, weather permitting. It holds something for everyone, no matter when they come, or for how long they walk.

There are two major sections to Boynton Canyon: a smaller section behind Enchantment Resort, and a larger section that goes to the right of Kachina Woman. As you look at the canyon, you see a solitary spire that appears to have a ball sitting on the top. This spire is called Kachina Woman, and it separates the two sections of Boynton Canyon.

Upon arrival at Boynton Canyon, park in the public lot. About 1/10 of a mile along the road is the entrance to "Enchantment Resort" which was built within the smaller section, or extension of Boynton. To walk this part of the canyon, follow the trail marked FS #47. It takes you around the resort and into a very beautiful, peaceful and protected area. It takes about an hour to walk the full length of this section. Because it is a box canyon, you will have to return the way you came in. So, stay alert to the need for another hour to return to the parking lot. You do not have to walk to the end of the trail to receive the gifts of Boynton. They come even by sitting in the parking lot.

One of the rock guardians in Boynton Canyon

While in this part of the canyon, observe how alive the rocks are with Indian vibrations. Look for the cliff dwellings high above you. The rock surfaces form silhouettes, faces of animals and different symbols. Look for the monkey head as you walk into this part of the canyon. It is incredible! It stands like a guard or sentry protecting the canyon.

You will see many different varieties of animal life while in this part of the canyon. Look for the different birds, as well as butterflies, deer, and coyote to name a few. Life is active and present here, which is why this ares is so perfect to collect thoughts, feelings, and ideas about living, and believing that you can change how you live. Let yourself just enjoy where you are and the good feeling that comes while in this canyon.

Medicine wheel in Boynton Canyon

To envelop yourself in another awesome view, walk around Kachina Woman and discover the larger section of the canyon. It is to the right of the parking lot, about 1/2 to 3/4 of a mile past Kachina Woman. There is a trail that will take you around Kachina Woman into this part of Boynton. It follows the telephone lines for about half a mile and then the trail splits. You will want to go to the left. As you are walking, you will see an immense Indian silhouette to your left. When that silhouette is directly across from you, you will be able to see the entirety of the canyon, bordered by magnificent rock walls that stretch to the open sky. It takes about 45 minutes to walk the full length of this section of Boynton Canyon.

Indian head silhouette

Your own identity; in the scope of this universe, becomes part of your journey as you view the immense rock fortresses. These fortresses are very protective and you feel safe enough to listen to your inner guide and know that you can believe what you hear. The vortex energy in this area takes you deep into yourself and how you feel about your life and the way you are living it. It helps you see the inner causes for some of your life's circumstances and presents logical solutions to making life positive and peaceful.

The view and sense of magnitude is still enjoyable when you turn around and begin walking out of the canyon. The panorama that was behind you walking into the canyon is now blessing your presence by being the view that guides you back out.

You take on a sense of self balance and inner strength as you walk this part of the canyon. The balance of self then helps you to open psychically to your clairvoyant and intuitive abilities. Enjoy the day in Boynton. Let past lives, forgotten memories and intuitive experiences unfold.

Boynton Canyon is magic regardless of which part you walk. The ground is soft and it seems as if you glide along the trails. Magic is expressed through the Spirit entities, fairies, little people and animal spirits that are present here. Notice how your voice carries. Feel the peacefulness of the energy through the melodic sound of your voice echoing through the canyon.

Boynton Canyon is full of Indian life memories. You feel the presence of the dwellers as you look at the canyon walls and explore ancient cliff dwellings in this area. The energy here awakens our belief in our own mortality. We sense lives lived and changed, and now the canyon holds the memories of those lives. We realize that we are responsible for our own existence and what we do with it. Each day takes on a new and very special significance.

As you walk either section, let go and center into yourself. Realize your own importance and recognize your life and how you would like to change it. At Boynton, you become aware of your own receptivity. You explore your life and try to create a peacefulness and open connection within yourself.

Norm C., an engineer, had been observing himself while walking through Boynton Canyon one day.

"I was really working on my beliefs about giving and receiving this one particular time I was walking through the canyon. I found myself totally connected with the feeling of the canyon. I could feel the magic of this place. I stopped in the river bed to try and pick up on the energy of the stones there. As I was trying to "receive" my lesson of the day, a woman walked up to me and started a conversation. We talked for over an hour and I felt so connected to her, the canyon, and the wholeness of it all while we talked. I was empowered! I was safe and I had a voice, something very new for me. There was no fight for space or to be heard. I saw that I could be open and vulnerable with someone. I think the magic of the Boynton walk helped me see this.

Later that day, I was given a Kachina doll. I was told that it symbolized all the things I had experienced earlier in the canyon. And this person knew nothing about my talk with the woman. Give and receive lessons were very prominent in that day. At first I was a little frightened. The space that I thought was private and protected could actually be "picked up" or recognized by others.

The contrast in my feelings about those two experiences really got me thinking. The coincidences about fear and safety were actually magical for me. I began looking at what safety really is for me in my everyday life. As I started doing that, I realized that this is exactly what Boynton is about! It's the daily walk of life where you connect, learn, and grow, and you create your own safe spaces along the way. What a realization it was for me!"

Boynton Canyon

Boynton assists you to let go of your fears of self disclosure or your fears of inadequacy. Here, allow balance to come into the self and accept yourself as you are: the best possible vehicle for this earth journey. Receptivity is a gift you give yourself; you awaken your own self magic, and allow yourself to know that life can be peaceful, beautiful and full of living in every moment. The present is important in Boynton because of the intenseness of past living here. You awaken to your own past lives while in this canyon.

The magnetic energy of Boynton Canyon helps you to see how slippery life can be and that you can easily walk unconsciously through your days. It helps you to wake up to where in your life you are unconscious. The magnetic energy is also the sensitive, caring, inner energy that takes you deeper into yourself and others. It creates intimacy and keeps the gifts of surprise, the treasures, symbols, and coincidences of life coming to the surface.

The electric part of Boynton helps us to experience these treasures and incorporate them into understandable language and experience. It assists us to actively work with these gifts of the unknown. While in Boynton, you may feel the need to walk and keep moving because of the electric energy. As you move, you may also find yourself contemplating past lives, lessons or experiences because your subconscious has been stirred by the magnetic energy present. Allowing the energies to blend will create pictures, or ideas for dealing with life now. You will feel your own power. Discover that which has been holding you back and realize the strength to release those things as you walk. This is the blend of electric and magnetic energy.

People may have very different experiences in Boynton Canyon. One couple, Karen and Phil, found themselves appreciating Boynton from different viewpoints because of these energy differences. Karen plugged into the magnetic energy and remembers "It gave me the awareness of my past that ties me down, and I did feel fear as I began my walk into Boynton." Phil on the other hand, connected with the electric part of Boynton and began his walk with a totally upbeat attitude. "It was like nothing was wrong while in Boynton. I had a sense of euphoria and actually got caught up in the feeling that everything was alright." Boynton brings to the surface our daily life lessons. Both Karen and Phil began walking lessons from their lives, but with their eyes open; which is what the vortex energy of Boynton helps awaken.

Boynton is where the "how to" of life begins, where you begin to talk, to touch the ground and the trees; where concepts become activated and real. Symbols come alive. Remember these symbols and you will see them all around you, as they can be anywhere in the canyon. Clairvoyance and third eye experiences are common in this vortex. Flow with that which feels good and appropriate for you and your beliefs. However, always use discretion when processing information from unknown sources. Remember that many spirits reside in the canyon and that they are not all necessarily of the highest vibration or intent. Just as in the walk of life, all people are not all of the highest vibration or intent. This is an area where real people lived. They had many different lives and experiences. Pay attention and stay alert so as to be able to understand the information and energy around you.

At Boynton, you will reconnect with the earth. The other vortexes took you off the earth, took you into yourself, or up into the sky. This one brings you gently back into your walk. The purpose of this place is for you to touch the earth so as to live and complete life's lessons. You will feel the energy more strongly in some spots than in others. This is another great lesson in being aware. Life holds different experiences in each moment; learn to flow with them. Through this flow, you will be at peace and walk openly. Boynton is the initiation walk into present day through which you free yourself. It could be called the "Freedom Initiation Walk" because of how you become aware of yourself in a very concrete way that helps you release your fears of life.

Trail in Boynton Canyon

Questions To Be Answered At Boynton Canyon

This is the place of balance and gives the ability to see that which has been holding you back. One can experience release and movement here. Keep in mind that you are in Boynton Canyon while contemplating the following questions. Be sure and write your thoughts below.

1. What is freedom to you?

....
....
....
....
....
....
....

2. What is involved in your being free?

....
....
....
....
....
....
....

3. What needs to happen for you to free yourself?

    ....
    ....
    ....
    ....
    ....
    ....
    ....

4. How do you celebrate self freedom?

    ....
    ....
    ....
    ....
    ....
    ....
    ....

5. What symbols, animals, or visions have revealed themselves to you on this freedom walk?

    ....
    ....
    ....
    ....
    ....
    ....
    ....

A Walk Through Boynton Canyon

A Walk In The Canyon Meditation Exercise

There is incredible life in this canyon, life of many kinds. Because of this, you may want to elicit your spirit guides to support and protect you while walking the canyon. It will be helpful to take a moment to quiet yourself and ask for their support. Hold to a state of mind that is willing to receive from the canyon and then let it expand to a willingness to receive from the universe. It will take up to two hours to walk the canyon. Enjoy the beauty and vortex energy of blend and balance that is present here.

A walk through the canyon is important because it frees you of the past and solidifies new understandings. While on your walk into the canyon, keep in mind that you want to look for symbols. Take the energy of the vortex into the center of your crown, down through your feet until you find yourself balancing into the earth. Use the vortex energy to make the connection. Begin your walk.

Answer the following questions about your walk.

1. Was your heart open to receiving while walking into the canyon? How did it feel?

   ....
   ....
   ....
   ....

2. What did you receive and how was it significant for you?

   ....
   ....
   ....
   ....

3. How do you accept that which you receive in your life?

   ....
   ....
   ....
   ....

8. What symbols showed on your walk?

   ....
   ....
   ....
   ....

Personal Observations While in Boynton Canyon

Kachina Woman

"The Goddess"

    Within the walls of Boynton Canyon, standing as a fortress, is Kachina Woman. She is a single spire of electric energy, a symbol of peace and serenity, of personal empowerment, as well as of standing aware amongst the confusions of earth. Because she is electric in nature, she is a place where one connects directly with the vortex energy. It is not an underground vibration, but one that moves directly into your body. Walk around until you arrive at the right spot, take in the energy and then let it back out. This creates a sense of empowerment.

Kachina is keeper of the earth in many ways and is much like a spirit guide, but she comes from the world of stone. Her electric energy allows you to realize that you can receive from the universe your wishes and dreams. She represents the Goddess energy and the place where you can feel a true sense of yourself, be heard and receive without fear. One need not fear any lack in the self because a sense of self power occurs here. Rebecca, a counselor from Manhattan, Kansas, had an experience that helped her become aware of her own power. She felt her Goddess self awaken. She remembers:

"I found what I call a power chair while at Kachina Woman. It felt quite comfortable and I began to meditate. I started to feel empowered with a sense of self worth and confidence. When I opened my eyes I was captivated by the valley below, and I felt like the queen. This filled me with a sense of Goddess energy and triggered my fear of the power of the Goddess within me. I finally became aware of my greatest fear, the fear of my own power. I was afraid I might misuse my power and hurt either others or myself.

As I was reflecting on this, I turned around and became aware of the huge mountain (Kachina Woman) behind me. I could feel her power and realized she was more powerful than me. This helped keep me humble. I began to feel more a part of all things, not more powerful, or higher than, just a part of all.

When I first sat in the chair and was feeling like the queen, I thought I was more powerful because I was higher than everyone else. But, when I turned around and felt Kachina, I recognized that there is always something more powerful. As I was soaking in the immenseness of this lesson, some hikers asked me if this area was male or female energy. This immediately triggered my fear that I may not know the answer. Knowing this was my opportunity to see how much I had learned about power, I decided to address my power in speaking the truth. I sensed the protection of speaking the truth and through that you are not harming or hurting anyone; in fact it becomes wisdom in motion."

In the walk of life where much is unknown, Kachina is steadfast in reminding us that trust, faith, prayer and change are always available and easily accessible. She invites prayers and requests for support. In launching those prayers, she takes them and steadfastly holds them. You know your prayers are heard and she will respond with insightful information that often includes past life understandings. Because she is electric in nature, change can come just through the recognition of the information presented. She offers understanding to life's daily dramas and teaches you how to actively trust and have faith.

Kachina Exercise of Prayer

Kachina is a place of magic and miracles. It is a place of peace, and she is the supporter. While here, and a part of Kachina Woman's energy, put forth your personal prayers or requests.

Some examples of prayers or requests are:
    Letting go of confusion in your life
    Allowing yourself to receive what is divinely yours
    Setting forth your desires, hope and dreams, etc.

Write a prayer or request for self acceptance or for support of your desires using Kachina's energy. Ask for a symbol of that support. Know that your prayer is heard and that you are supported.

Write down your prayer and what you hear in response from the energy. You may find it difficult to remember if you do not write it down.

Answer the following questions after writing your prayer or request:

1.   How do you accept yourself?

....
....
....
....

2. What is support to you?

....
....
....
....
....
....

3. What are your desires?

....
....
....
....
....
....
....

4. What will you do to support yourself and you desires?

....
....
....
....
....
....
....

My Prayer or Request to Kachina Woman

My Observations While at Kachina Woman

Schnebly Hill

"The Place of Universal Healing"

Driving down a dusty, bumpy road, not sure if you will even find the special spot, could dampen your sense of adventure. However, let the explorer in you emerge and keep going, it will be worth it. Look at this bumpy road as the road of life which contains many unlearned lessons. It is bumpy, full of pitfalls and sometimes you want to give up, but if you watch for the bumps and ruts, the lessons get easier. You learn to be observant, to become aware of where you are going and the answers come, as on Schnebly Hill. Just like the answers to life's questions, Schnebly Hill appears to be hidden from those who do not know how to read the road map.

Park by the flat rock on your right. You will see the open space and then the clump of trees to the left. Unsure of the correct path, put faith in your hip pocket and begin your journey. There are no markers to tell you the way. There are few, if any, people to assure you that you are heading in the right direction. And lastly, you encounter a herd of cows and think that you are in a farmer's pasture. These possibilities are just like life, wherein there are many things that can shake your confidence in yourself. Head for the clump of trees.

As you pass through the clump of trees, notice the dry river bed. You are very close now to the entrance of Schnebly Hill and the sacred energy it holds. As the trees end, you enter the swirling, spiraling energy of this place. The original medicine wheel, which contained wheel upon wheel, is now gone, but a very beautiful and simple wheel has birthed in its place. Medicine wheels seem to grow here. The energy is so chaotic and swirling in nature that the wheels become focusing tools. The wheels symbolize the sacred connection between heaven and earth.

Schnebly Hill pasture friend

A sense of silence and awe fills you. You feel eternity in this spot, as if time stands still, or never existed at all. The feeling of God, Source, or All That Is, envelops you. Your beliefs about the meaning and purpose of life stir. You can remain in this lower section or continue exploring the many areas of Schnebly Hill. When you are ready to continue, let yourself be pulled by the universal force. You will see a trail and it will guide you into another clump of trees, more rocks, another dry river bed and into another portal to eternity. Let intuition guide you as to where to connect. This area is vast and holds many spots to search your soul. One woman saw it as a hot air balloon and at the same time saw it as fast moving white water. Another saw it as the place to connect to the universe, creatures, heaven and earth.

A perfect spot to search your dreams

Schnebly Hill is not considered to be one of the major vortexes, but we believe, through our personal experience, that this area holds something very special. You want to be alone and become one with the energy. You do not want to talk but rather to let go of all thoughts and focus on your soul. You ask questions, such as what is the meaning of life, where did we come from, and where are we going. On Schnebly Hill, the whole picture of life and self and the universe seems easy to grasp.

You will not experience limitations of any kind here. The whole picture unfolds because the energy of Schnebly Hill does not have a direction; it swirls. Be careful of your footing because you could easily fall. The energy reaches into your unconscious, into your unknowns, and moves those unknowns. It is very much a blend of Bell and Cathedral but from a universal perspective. Cathedral presents the unknowns from the heart line and Bell moves whatever is present. Schnebly takes this combination and reaches into the unknown or unremembered parts of the soul and brings those issues to the surface so that you can consciously realize what was hidden and then let them go. You receive soul healing through this movement of energy.

Anne E., a legal secretary from Portland, Oregon, found Schnebly to have incredible depth. It disconnected her from the present and put her into another world, an altered dimension, or some kind of time warp. Through that experience, she was able to reach her soul. "The depth of energy was so great that I was able to get in touch with another level of my soul. It was like staring into a small hole that opened into a cavern. When you step into the cavern there is an expansive feeling of depth. The depth of Schnebly opened me up so that I could see the depth of me."

We have seen many people experience that which is called "Soul Reconnection" at Schnebly Hill. This happens when you bring back into consciousness a part of your soul that was lost or unattainable until now. Schnebly helps open the spot within you to allow that wholeness to happen. Here, you gather the courage to look for those lost parts of self and then consciously bring them forward. Once forward you are able to incorporate them into daily living.

Anne also remembers a reconnection that she experienced while on Schnebly.

"I remember laying face down and going deep into the earth. I was there to find anything that was ready to become alive in me again. I found my little girl. She did exist. I was actually there. I had heard people talk about their inner child before but had no idea what they were talking about, much less think that I also had an inner child that I needed to get in touch with.

The energy of Schnebly was safe and seemed to help me move deep into the earth, or into myself actually. It created the circumstances for me to have this experience. I opened to feeling there. It was a turning point in my soul's progression. I knew I was different immediately after that experience. I felt numb, yet tingly all over. It was like post traumatic stress syndrome, or like I had just stepped off a battlefield. I could not go backwards from that point on. I had opened myself up and had to keep going forward. This new me felt good. I felt real and whole."

    This is one reason why you come to Schnebly, to find your wholeness. This place helps you understand that the earth is part of the universe and that you are not separate. As you become part of the swirling, you realize that you can be one with everyone and everything. It is your opportunity to understand the blend of soul and physical.

    Schnebly energy is wonderful for moving physical pains, emotional sorrows, fears and angers from the body as well as from the soul. This is a place where you can reach into issues and allow self forgiveness to melt them away. Because this is a universal energy, it helps you to see the whole picture without any judgment, anger or fear. You see things as facts and truths only. You will leave Schnebly feeling wonderful! This place touches your soul. It is immense and vast in what it can do to help us achieve wholeness.

    As Schnebly is a place of universal energy, you may see not only past earth life experiences but also past soul life experiences. It can take you into your original soul self, before any earth connection, before any physical life connections. With this knowledge, you can begin to piece together the total picture of who you are by who you have been from the beginning of self.

    Schnebly Hill can help you to connect with the other side of life, the spirit side of life. The invisible worlds are better understood in Schnebly energy because you are able to see the whole picture. This is a place of self expansion which takes you past your own self-imposed limits. You see that you do not need to limit what you believe or feel and you recognize that you can learn more, allow more, and accept more.

It is easy to vision while on Schnebly because you let go of earthly, physical problems and expand into your potential. You see a greater picture of yourself and this greater picture becomes your "vision of self." Everything seems possible in Schnebly energy.

A heavenly view from the upper section of Schnebly

Questions to be Answered at Schnebly Hill

1. Describe how you experience trust in your life.

2. How is vulnerability a strength as well as a weakness for you?

3. Describe how you experience the unknown in your life.

4. How are your emotions a strength as well as a weakness for you?

....
....
....
....

5. Describe how you experience personal wisdom.

....
....
....
....

6. How is patience a strength as well as a weakness for you?

....
....
....
....

7. Describe how you experience inspiration in your life.

....
....
....
....

8. How is chaos a strength as well as a weakness for you?

....
....
....
....

The Wheel of Life Exercise

This exercise is to help you to recognize the lessons that you are presently learning. It will also help you to understand the qualities you have that will help you to learn those lessons. Through awareness and self-forgiveness you can be non-resistant and set yourself free of their control over you. Lessons are learned once we are able to be non-resistant and accept them for the message they present.

Medicine wheels at Schnebly Hill

Directions:

1. Find a spot on Schnebly that the energy feels right for you. There are many areas to choose from here. Center into yourself and begin to touch into that special spot for you. Either use an existing medicine wheel or construct one of your own to use as an aid to getting in touch with your lessons through this exercise. You will also get in touch with the strengths and qualities you now carry. The medicine wheel is a beautiful tool to focus on specific aspects of yourself.

2. Standing at the "Southgate" draw in the energy of that direction.

3. Open up to the strengths and qualities within you that it represents. You may want to look through the "Strengths and Lessons of each Direction" on pages 154 -157 to help you recognize your strengths.

4. Recognize any body responses that you may have as you are standing at the Southgate. Let your body fill with the qualities of that direction. You could try filling yourself with the qualities that you may not recognize as strengths within you. Try opening up to the potential of those qualities as part of you.

5. Take a few minutes to meditate on any lessons that you may have that are connected with the Southgate.

6. Once you are aware of these lessons, focus on your strengths and let those strengths show you how to release the lessons. Is your strength also your lesson?

   For example, innocence or vulnerability can be gifts. They can present a willingness to accept things as they are, present an openness to letting others know who you are. As a lesson, you could be naive and unaware. You may be hurt because you are too open with others. We strive for balance in innocence where we are willing to be open and share ourselves, but are aware of how others are receiving our openness. We can be vulnerable yet aware. This is non-resistance in action. Innocence and vulnerability are only two of the strengths or lessons of the Southgate. Study the list to determine which pieces fit you best.

7. Continue taking in the strengths of the Southgate until you can feel this balance and sense of non-resistance to the lessons.

8. Say a prayer of self acceptance for the gifts of the Southgate.

   To continue, say a prayer of self acceptance for your gifts of innocence and willingness to be open and trusting. Also say a prayer of self forgiveness for how innocence may have caused you problems or pain.

9. Continue on to the next gate, repeating the above directions.

10. Once you have completed your circle, stand in the middle of the wheel and create a prayer honoring Father Sky and Mother Earth. Complete this exercise with an acceptance of yourself and your wholeness created through this experience.

11. Be kind to the environment and once you are complete with this exercise disassemble your medicine wheel. Return the land to the same condition you found it.

Schnebly Hill

The Strengths and Lessons of each Direction Through the Medicine Wheel

Each direction of the wheel has specific qualities and strengths, as well as lessons that correspond to it. As you are standing and contemplating the self in each direction, keep in mind the specific strengths and lessons to see if any of them are part of you. This is your opportunity to acknowledge them.

South Direction: Red

The South is about the child within, as your adult-self walks through life. It is what you need to trust in yourself and others. The color red has been used to symbolize the south because it contains the energies of vitality, strength, and earth when used with the directions through the wheel.

Look for strengths and lessons about:
1. relationships
2. trust
3. innocence
4. vulnerability
5. strength or courage
6. your environment
7. self-determination/will
8. your child self
9. humor

West Direction: Black

This direction is about the internal solution to your present life challenges. It is about emotions and how we bring the parts of self together. The color black has been used to symbolize the west because it contains the energies of emotions, looking into the void, spiritual renewal and dream work when used with the directions through the wheel.

Look for strengths and lessons about:
1. introspection
2. shamanic journeys
3. psychic work
4. sacred dreams
5. self balance
6. compassion
7. imagery
8. emotions
9. the adolescent self
10. rights of passage
11. death/rebirth

North Direction: White

The North teaches you how to spiritually apply and integrate the strengths and lessons of the other directions. North is the key to walking in wisdom, knowing the teacher within, and connecting to the higher self's purpose and intention. The color white has been used to symbolize the north because it contains the energies of truth, symbology, wisdom and purity when used with the directions through the wheel.

Look for strengths and lessons about:
1. patience
2. teaching
3. the purpose and understanding of symbols, rituals or ceremonies
4. body work
5. money
6. possessions
7. learning
8. your adult self
9. the logical wisdom behind things
10. spirit
11. prayer
12. wisdom

East Direction: Yellow

The East reveals where your spiritual strength lies. It also indicates the direction your spiritual path is taking. It can also reveal the major challenge to seeing clearly in your present position. The color yellow has been used to symbolize the east because it contains the energies of thought, creativity, illumination, spiritual power and focus when used with the directions through the wheel.

Look for strengths and lessons about:
1. inspiration
2. creative ideas
3. chaos into balance
4. psychic/spiritual work
5. thought/mental work
6. defining the abstract
7. the higher self
8. the universal self
9. looking at the "big picture" - gestalt
10. illumination
11. mental powers
12. beliefs and values

Characteristics of the Wheel

Each direction has specific characteristics, animals, emotions, ages of life, vibrations or tones, and colors associated with it. Below is listed one example of characteristics that correspond to each direction:

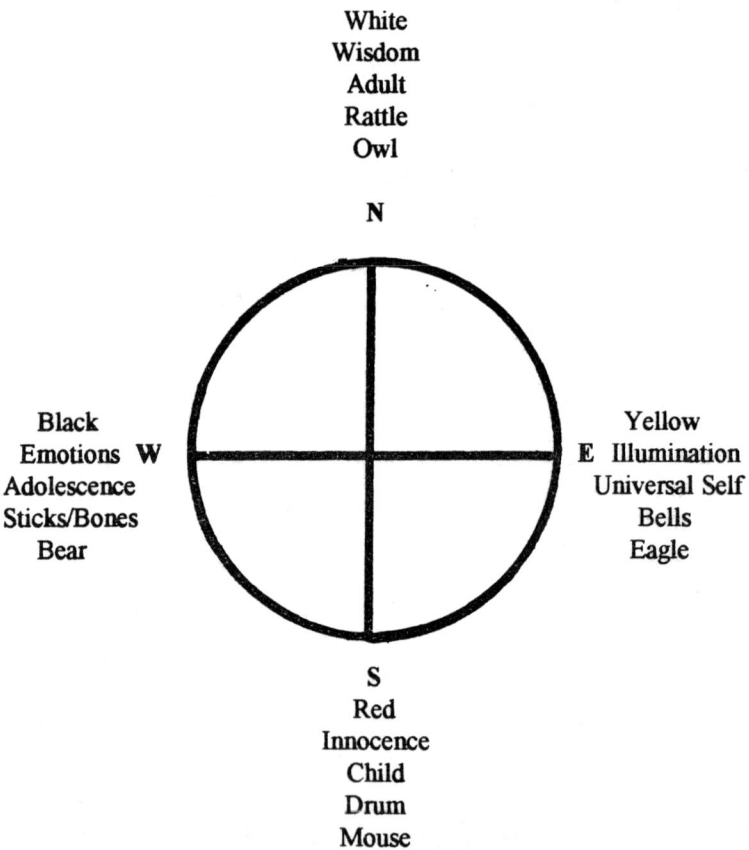

Use the above medicine wheel diagram for ideas of what to focus on while standing at each direction or "gate."

Color Meditation

Cleansing Meditation Exercise

You may want to record this meditation so you can concentrate on it. This meditation is best done in the area that contains the medicine wheel, which is situated on the first level of Schnebly as you come through the clump of trees.

Part I:

Lay face down, relax, and begin to touch the rock under you. Begin to breathe in Schnebly, take in the smells, the wind, the energy that floats in the air, and as you breath it in, move it through your chakras into the earth. Each breath will move you deeper into the earth.
(PAUSE)
Let yourself reach back, back through all time, back through all that is known to you, so that you are not connected to anything that you know. Back into this earth, back into the heavens, back into the universe, back through all time. Feel the motion of the swirling moving you back until you no longer have connection to this planet, no connection to memories of this earth. You are free, you are gliding, floating, floating with purpose.
(PAUSE)
In this free state, let go of anything held in your body, mind and spirit.
(PAUSE)

Part II:
Roll over onto your back and create a rainbow of chakra colors at the base of your spine. Include all the colors of your chakras: red, orange, yellow, green, blue, indigo and purple. Take a few minutes and allow yourself to fully see and feel these colors. Experience the sense of a rainbow of color.

(PAUSE)

This rainbow of color moves up your spine into the first chakra. Total awareness moves into your place of security. Total understanding of your security is now in this rainbow of color. Understand it, feel it, feel the security, the safety, the individuality of your first chakra. Allow this rainbow of color to move through the first and out into the universe above you.

(PAUSE)

Move the rainbow of color into your second chakra so that you are secure in accepting your emotions in balance. The rainbow of color floods the second chakra and it now bursts into the universe above you and it blends with the energy of the first so that your cloud of rainbow colors gets bigger above you.

(PAUSE)

Take the rainbow from your spine and move it into your third chakra. The security of the first, and the emotions of the second, help you to see your identity now, help you to see ego as a strength, action as a strength, and it grows and it builds in this third chakra. It moves anger and fear because the rainbow of color is perfect understanding. It moves through the third into the universe, into the universe above you and blends with the first and second to make a bigger cloud of more rainbow colors.

(PAUSE)
Take the rainbow into your heart. Let the rainbow flood the heart with color, color so vivid and so bright. You have never seen such brightness. And it brings with it the security, the emotions, and the strength of your ego to have compassion for yourself, to love yourself. This rainbow of color grows in your heart, and it moves out above you, blending with the cloud which now grows even bigger. It glows with the brightness of the rainbow colors, all blending together. See how bright and full it is.

(PAUSE)
Move the rainbow into your fifth chakra. Bring with it the strengths of your lower chakras and the awareness of the heart, so that your communication is perfectly clear. The rainbow presents that all knowledge can be communicated. As you feel the vibration of color in the throat, allow it to move out above you, blending with the cloud of color. The cloud of color grows, and it gets bigger and brighter.

(PAUSE)
And now from the reservoir in your spine, move the rainbow into your sixth chakra. Accept the rainbow of color. It takes the strengths of the lower chakras, the awareness and loving of the heart, and the ability to speak and hear, and it takes it into knowing, takes it into understanding and into seeing. The color grows in the sixth chakra, and the third eye begins to open and there is a pressure in your third eye as the color moves out. The rainbow of color blends with the cloud above you. Your knowingness is open. Your acceptance of self is open. You now know because you are in balance with yourself.

(PAUSE)
Move your rainbow into your seventh chakra, into your universal chakra. The rainbow of color fills your crown. It takes the strengths of the lower chakras, it takes the compassion of the heart, it takes the communication and hearing of the fifth, it takes the knowing of the sixth, and it blends them all into the seventh, where all makes sense, all is known, all is understood, and your entirety is blended. And it now moves out the crown and blends with the cloud of color above you.
(PAUSE)
This cloud of color grows and it is getting brighter and more beautiful. It is the power of self above you, but always connected to you. All growing, all a rainbow of color. And this rainbow cloud, through your strength, moves up to the universe, up to the heaven. Let it move, let it go to the universe, and let it go as high as it can go, but always still connected to you. Let the energy move and allow your rainbow colors light the way.
(PAUSE)
In the peace and beauty of the universe accept into your rainbow that which the universe offers you. Receive the gifts of the universe.
(PAUSE)
Bring your rainbow of color filled with the universal gifts back into your body. Accept the new lightness your rainbow contains. Take in the lightness and let your consciousness connect with it so that you can live this rainbow filled with these universal gifts every day.

A Soul's Journey...

You will journey to find the power of your spirit, as well as the powers that are guides to your spirit.

You may want to record this meditation so you can concentrate on it. This meditation is best done in the area above the medicine wheel. Continue on the trail past the medicine wheel, through another clump of trees and over a dry riverbed. Once through the trees, the space opens up. Go to your left and find a spot that feels right to you.

A Soul's Journey Meditation Exercise

Lay on your back so that you can blend with the earth. Connect into the rock, knowing that it cradles you with support and firmness. Be peaceful so that you can be open to the heavens and your guides.
(PAUSE)
Allow the blessings of this earth to be your protector, and know that this earth protector will always support you. In a gentle breath gather your essence, feel the essence within you, feel the essence of self glowing within the heart, filtering out of your body. It is the golden light of self glowing within, expanding and growing, and filling the edges of your form, expanding out from you, reaching into the sky.

(PAUSE)
Feel the golden light of self being freed from the body, moving out of the body, free, full of life. Breathe your spirit free.
(PAUSE)
Feel it reach the heavens, and the golden light grows, and it is strong, and it is firm because it is supported by the light of heaven.
(PAUSE)
Your golden light is supported by heaven, and it cradles your light, it cradles your essence, and it helps you keep moving higher and higher, supported by light, supported by the self's light.
(PAUSE)
Each breath moves you higher to heaven, freer from earth, yet always supported by the rock you lay on.
(PAUSE)
Allow your golden light to reach into the velvety darkness, into the voids within the heavens, into the spaces unknown in the heavens, reaching higher and higher in trust, supported by your light.
(PAUSE)
You are moving through the velvety darkness into a place, a temple, a meadow, a stream, a garden. Go with trust to this place that is calling you. Respond to the call within.
(PAUSE)
Allow the self to move to where you are drawn. Are there stairs, are there flowers, is there grass, is there dirt, is there water? Or is it just the heavens?
(PAUSE)
Allow yourself to roam this new place, this place of trust and truth and light, for it is a place you could call home

to your spirit, it is familiar, you know this place, you have been here hundreds and thousands of times. And you can feel the support from this place.
(PAUSE)
How brilliant are the colors? What is your appearance? Are you light, or are you in a form? How are your clothes if you are in a form? How does it feel to be in this temple of self, totally supported by light, totally safe in the lights of heaven? Continue to roam, look around, keep moving forward, taking a step, floating, moving forward through your garden, through your land, through your temple.
(PAUSE)
On the count of three you will turn around and there will be a Wise One waiting to speak with you. But now, keep walking, visit your home, know that you are safe and that at this moment you have invited in your Wise One to guide you, to support you, to be your journey friend.
(PAUSE)
One, two three! Turn around, meet your friend.
(PAUSE)
Look into the eyes of the soul of your friend. Do you know this friend? Do you trust this friend? What does this friend look like? Ask this friend what information he or she has for you.
(PAUSE)
Listen to the words of your friend - they carry a message for you, a message about your tomorrows and how to work with your own spirit.
(PAUSE)
Ask your Wise One, does he know God? Ask him to describe God in terms that you will understand.
(PAUSE)

Ask yourself, am I willing to accept my God? If any discomfort arises, ask permission to move it to the Wise One. He will support it until you transform it.
(PAUSE)
Ask your Wise One: Where is God?
(PAUSE)
Embrace your God, embrace your Wise One and bring them both home with you.
(PAUSE)
Breathe in the God light. Accept the light of God as your source, as the light within you, for they are one.
(PAUSE)
Know that you hold God. Know that you are God. You need not be separated from your God, from yourself. You walk light. Peace to you.

"Universal" medicine wheel on Schnebly Hill

Personal Observations
While at Schnebly Hill

Conclusion

A journey to the vortexes is moving and inspiring. It is an intense emotional experience. While in Sedona, you became part of a quaint art community and walked through some of the most beautiful landscape in the country. The red rocks with their deep, vibrating color came alive under your feet.

Along with being captivated by the beauty of the desert, you have many experiences such as time stopping, loss of appetite, immense energy surges, psychic experiences, vivid dreams, seeing color, energy or even spirit. These all affect your sense of perception and how you connect or ground yourself to your daily life. It is as if you had walked through the veil that separates you from the invisible world. Because the desert is so picturesque and awe inspiring, you may experience a plummeting of your emotions upon your return home. We call this post-Sedona blues. Try to be aware of this possibility. A little preparation will help soften the blow.

Keep looking at, and working with, what manifested on your journey. Do not forget what you learned once you return home. Create a daily focus from your Sedona journal of experiences. Look for symbols, messages, or inspirations about that daily focus. Write down your feelings and thoughts as they come forward. At the end of the week, meditate on how to blend what you received into your daily life. Ask how you can use this new energy in a real and helpful way. You could focus daily on one vortex and how the energy of that vortex can be lived at home. Look for messages to assist in discovering how to integrate the information that the vortex offers.

Be patient with yourself when you get home. Things are changing inside and you need to give yourself time to let those changes be real and usable. We have learned that it can take from three to six months to integrate a journey to Sedona. So take your time, move into daily activities slowly and utilize the new insights you have acquired.

If extreme emotions surface, realize that it is your body balancing the vortex changes with home living. You are full of new insights, as well as physical and chemical changes. Your body is slowly adjusting and may be doing it through emotional explosions. Be aware and prepare yourself if this begins to happen. In the sensitivity that you carry, you do not have to overpower another person to get them to hear or understand you, nor do you have to back away from situations which were frightening before. Be alert, listen, and respond. Understand that other people have not had the same experiences that you have. Realize that you are adjusting to a new you. You are working on fitting home to this new you. Take your time - **Be Patient!**

If you shared your time in Sedona with another, you will notice that there is a wonderful connection between you because you shared an experience of personal exploration. Those not on the journey may be confused by the words you speak. They may be unsure of where you are heading and of what you are doing. You may be unsure of them. Observe and listen. You will learn much more by listening, not just to the other people's words, but to the words inside of you.

Recognize the adjustments and that you are shifting dramatically in the beliefs that you carry about yourself. Accept what you receive and let yourself live the changes. Look at change as something valuable, as a moment of joy because whatever is changing is being replaced with something better. Recognize your emotions and how you are feeling, how you interact with other people, how you interact with your work places, with your family and all parts of your life. Accepting what you see opens you to integration, which in turns helps you see how to adjust and understand your new self. As you are adjusting do it through your new sight and not through your previous unenlightened eyes.

There is tremendous knowledge presented to you at the vortexes and you only need to accept it. Act on the new information and on those things that feel possible. Remember that you are seeing your world differently and incorporate this newness into your life. You can no longer approach your world as you did previously.

We hope that this book has helped to guide your steps on the path of spiritual awakening and enlightenment. Through vortex energy, we can all learn and grow, and become that which we are truly meant to be.

Journey well.

It was a good day

More Information About...

What should I bring?

Through our experiences, we have gathered a list of things that seem helpful while on the vortexes. You will want to look over the list and determine what might be helpful for you.

* Bring proper clothing for the season. We have been in snow at the end of April and it can rain at anytime, particularly in the springtime, July and August. The temperature varies greatly in the spring (March-May). Day temperatures can range from 50 to 80 degrees, with the lows down to 20 degrees at night. In the summer the temperature can go from lows of 60 up to 100 degrees. Dress accordingly.

* Do bring a water bottle that you can carry while on the vortexes. You will get very thirsty, not only from the hiking and heat, but also from the work you will be doing on yourself. Water helps clear impurities or negativities from the body.

* A backpack is a must if you want an easy way to carry your journal and supplies. Or try a fanny pack, which is wonderful for some people.

* A camera can provide visual memories of your experience. The scenery is beautiful here.

* You may not want to carry a video camera while on the vortexes. Once you are at the vortex, most of what you do will not be action oriented. We have also experienced that recorders will shut off while in the vortex energy.

* Bring a hat. It can get very warm and much time is spent outdoors where there is minimal shade. It will help prevent sunburn as well as potential heat stroke.

* A blanket or towel to sit on while doing your meditations and exercises is a good idea. It provides a little padding between you and the rocks. Some people bring folding or camping chairs. Inflatable cushions and chairs are light and easy to carry and can even fit in backpacks or attach to the outside of one.

* If you have special crystals, stones or objects, you may want to bring them. They can enhance your inner study. Crystals are a very good tool to help move the energy as well as to help clarify feelings and emotions.

* Bring a journal and pens.

* Suntan lotion and/or sun block is necessary if you burn easily. You are in Arizona and it gets warm.

* Good shoes for walking and doing minimal climbing. We have found that hiking boots can make a real difference on your feet and ankles. It is up to you how intense the climbing will be. To get to the vortexes, the walks are little more than a short hike. When you first see the vortexes they appear to be far away. However, it takes only a few minutes to reach them.

* Do bring a swimsuit. Time between vortexes can be spent in the pool or hot tub area. You will want to wash off each vortex energy before going to the next one. You should not mix the energies. This is one reason some people get confused while in vortex energy. If you are not comfortable swimming, you can wash off the energy by taking a hot shower.

* If you have a favorite incense you may want to bring it. Sometimes incense can connect us to our inner selves and becomes a good focusing tool. Be sure and take any unburned incense with you when you leave the vortex. We want to maintain a clean environment.

* You may want to bring a tape recorder to record your dreams or experiences while on the vortexes, except for on Cathedral where "silence is golden." You may also want to record any conversations you have with others.

Proper Breathing

It is important to understand breath and how to work with it while on the vortexes. Breath connects you with the earth energy and your own power. This connection helps you to be present in your body, to help you focus and therefore connect to self feelings. You want to establish a self-rhythm which can take 2 or 3 minutes. You will know you have established your rhythm when you feel consciously connected to it. It will have a meditative quality.

In-Breath:
Visualize and then feel the breath going into the belly. Feel as if you are a pitcher of water filling up from the belly, through the chest, into the arms and shoulders and all the way to the top of your head. Through the In-Breath feel the body inside. Feel where you are tense, tight, soft, hard, aching, or numb. Count to seven while taking in the breath. Hold the breath and slowly release to the count of seven.

Out-Breath
See and feel the body releasing the breath from the top of the head down to the belly. The out-breath is the surrender. It allows the self to let go. Become aware of how the body feels after the exhale.

Repeat the In-breath, Out-breath process.

The Chakra System

Chakras are energy points in our physical bodies. They help us understand and deal with our worlds. Chakras are channels for the energy activated by our feelings and thoughts. They are guidelines to the levels of feeling that we have and to what we create in ourselves. For example, they connect our feelings to our sense of security, or they connect our thoughts with our words. The interaction of energies helps us make decisions as well as create a comfortable exchange with others.

Diagram of Chakra Centers

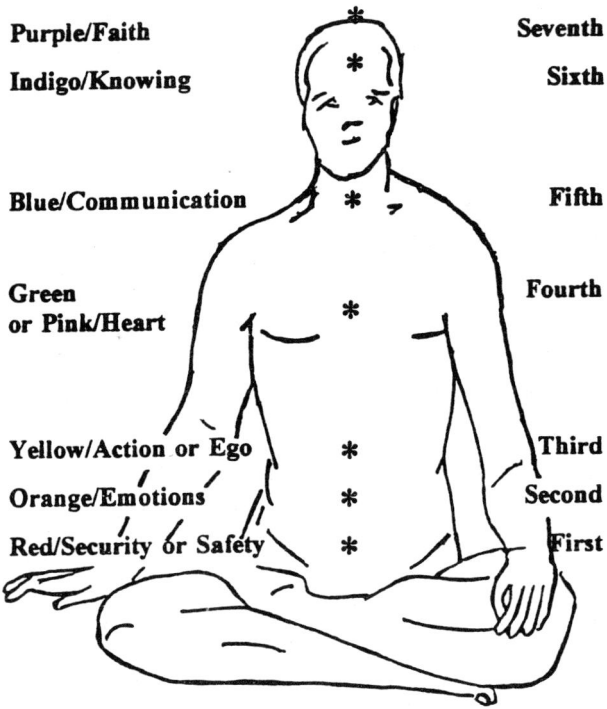

Chakra Descriptions

Chakra I: *(Red)* This center is where you establish your foundation as a physical person and begin to function at an earthly level. This is where you connect or ground to the earth. Personal survival and security are important and once established you begin to venture out and explore personal identity.

Chakra II: *(Orange)* Your center of emotions and feeling. The place where you begin to recognize that you exist among others. You realize that you can learn and exist through pleasure or pain. It is your choice.

Chakra III: *(Yellow)* Your ego center. The place of "I" in a balanced, living way. The action chakra where movement helps this center becomes balanced and flowing. You recognize self confidence and are able to accept new challenges.

Chakra IV: *(Green for healing of the heart, and Pink for the love energy in the heart)* This is the center of love and awareness coming from an unconditional place. You are detached from emotion and are able to see and observe the world around you from a different perspective - one of compassion and acceptance.

Chakra V: *(Blue)* The center of communication, referring to both speaking and hearing. You begin to let go of physical experiences once you are in the fifth. You begin opening up to connection in a spiritual sense. You hear spirit voices and even find yourself expressing words that do not seem to be coming from you directly. This is where you exchange energy through words, and with patience allow yourself to listen from a compassionate, unconditional spot.

Chakra VI: *(Indigo)* The third eye. The place of inner knowing, clairvoyance (the seeing with your inner eyes) and intuition. You could see visions of the past, present and also future. This center does not exist in time or have limits. All information is available through the balance of this center.

Chakra VII: *(Purple)* Your crown is the door opening center to the universe. Faith is strong and a part of this center. Thought is created in its purest form here. All is known in the seventh. You become less aware of self and more aware of everything as part of the whole picture. You understand that you are a small piece of that whole, but as important as every other piece of that picture. Nothing is more important or better than anything else in the seventh. All is one.

Dreams and Vortex Energy

In Sedona energy, dreams are abundant and vivid, yet sometimes slippery. As we have previously discussed, the magic of Sedona speaks in imagery, symbology and quiet remembrances. Dreams offer access to the lovely realm of genius in our night journeys. As we have mentioned, while working with vortex energy, clear intent and purpose support the gathering of information.

We suggest that each night you ask for dreams that support your journey. Write down your memories when you awaken. It is important for you to collect any dream pieces as well as weird symbols and story lines. Dreams tend to unravel from the end to the beginning, so write down whatever is produced. There may or may not be a continuity to the logic of the information. Do not judge it. Allow it to be realized, explored and incorporated. There may be past life remembrances as well as connections to your present in these dream realms.

We have included a sample form for an easy way to record the nightly puzzle pieces while in Sedona.

Dream Time

Date _____

Day Notes:
What was the day like? Were there any special thoughts, feelings, experiences, conflicts, insights, fears, etc...

Actual Dream:

Record your dream in present tense as you remember it.

About Your Dream:

When you awoke from your dream, what were your feelings?

....
....
....
....
....
....

Describe any outstanding symbols, characters, settings, colors, metaphors, etc.

....
....
....
....
....
....

State the theme of your dream in one or two sentences.

....
....
....
....
....

What do you think your dream is saying to you about yourself?

....
....
....
....
....
....
....
....
....
....
....

Does your dream tie into any of the experiences you have had while in Sedona?

....
....
....
....
....
....
....
....
....
....
....

Animals on the Vortexes

During our visits to Sedona and the vortexes we have encountered various animals. They always have a message for us. We have learned their "language" through our interactions with them. We have included the general theme of their messages. Read them and see if they have meaning for you. Try to make this general information specific to you and to your lessons of the moment. If you encounter other animals, try to decipher their message to you.

Ant: Represents patience and success through effort. Realize that your dreams are being built right now, one step at a time. You will always have what is yours at the appropriate time. Represents wisdom in work, order, and industriousness. Ant is social, especially in regards to its own community. It harnesses power to redesign and recreate its life.
Ask yourself: Am I laying a good foundation? Am I accomplishing tasks and real goals and harnessing my true power?

Bat: Transition and intuition. Death and rebirth. Bat represents the release of what no longer fits so that new growth can emerge; the birth of something new within yourself. Do not resist the flow of change, it is inevitable. We must change and grow to be alive. Bat shows facing your greatest fears and preparing for change. It presents promises of empowerment by rising above what is there.
Ask yourself: Is there anything ready for release? What fears are getting in the way of change and rebirth?

Bee: Fertility, the promise of accomplishment of short term goals. It is about the here and now and the ability to fulfill our dreams.
Ask yourself: Am I accomplishing what I truly want to accomplish? What is truly fulfilling to me?

Butterfly: Shows the process of change or transformation. Through self study, you emerge from your cocoon of fear and doubt as a beautiful being able to soar with a new awareness of self. Butterfly helps gracefully move you to the next level of awareness. Accept with grace the shifts. Stay in flow and listen for inspiration about change and let it come gracefully and easily.
Ask yourself: What important issues are confronting me at this moment? How much joy is there in my life?

Coyote: The trickster, who often fools himself. Be aware of events crashing down around you. They could fall leaving you wondering about what happened. The signs and clues are present and waiting for you to see them. You have created these situations to fulfill a purpose. What is it? Because the coyote is the trickster, as well as the jokester, look for the humor in your situations, which will help you understand and accept that coyote can even help move you into completing your lessons.
Ask yourself: If things are tumbling down around me, what am I not looking at?

Deer: Compassion, gentleness, peace, love and centeredness are all part of Deer energy. Look for peaceful, gentle ways to nurture and love yourself and others. Let go of push. Connect with God or with the universe and release any negativities. Let universal guidance create the changes necessary. Let Go and Let God!
Ask yourself: Am I being gentle on myself? Or are am I pushing myself or others too hard?

Dog: Friend, protector. Guardian to your secrets and person. They are givers in spite of their needs. Look at your own sense of loyalty to yourself or to those you love, or to those you serve.
Ask yourself: How loyal have I been? Am I showing unconditional love? Am I receiving it? Am I protecting my space and creating comfortable boundaries? Am I sharing my life openly with those close to me?

Dolphin: There is a great deal of dolphin energy present in Sedona; therefore, we have chosen to include the dolphin in this section. You may come across the sense of dolphins, see pictures, or statues of them while here. You may feel they are calling to you. Their meaning is: The breath of life. The helper to the release of emotions. Dolphin helps bring forward our feelings. It reminds us to breathe. We receive universal life force through our breathing. Dolphin reminds us to take into our bodies the invisible energy and let it become part of us. Pay attention to your body rhythm. Go into your body and feel what is here.
Ask yourself: Am I bringing in new possibilities, feelings, and experiences that offer me joy and inspiration?

Eagle: Expansion of life. Eagle represents state of grace achieved through hard work and understanding of one's personal power. Take heart, have courage. Look above where you have been and know that you can reach higher.
Ask yourself: Am I openly involved with creativity and the expression of my greatest passions? Am I willing to rise above my old patterns and boxes to get a new perspective of possibilities? Is my warrior self willing to bring balance in my life by eliminating the weak and shallow aspects?

Fox: Skillfully able to adapt to change; to become one with your surroundings and your lessons, fears, doubts, etc. Become the observer of yourself and those around you. Feel the energy around you. Do not just listen to the words that you hear. Observe all things in your surroundings. This will help you know where events are heading and you can then be prepared for them.
Ask yourself: Am I camouflaging myself to observe and utilize my magical skills of perception and adaptation?

Frog: Represents clearing, transformation, abundance, and fertility. It releases negativity from the environment and supports new life and harmony.
Ask yourself: Where do I need clearing and cleansing in my life? Where am I anxious or empty in my body? What will give me a sense of harmony?

Hawk: Represents messages and protection. Look for the symbols, the signals, the messages that are all around you, in the obvious as well as in the hidden. Look for the overall picture of present dilemmas. Anything could be hiding a clue to life right now, or to the future. Analyze how the clues fit.
Ask yourself: How do things happening around me fit into my dilemmas?

Hummingbird: Represents joy, curiosity, freedom, heart opening. This bird has the capacity to fly in any direction, reflecting the ability to look backward and bring the best forward.
Ask yourself: What is beckoning me to explore more beauty in my life? How can I release judgment and move into a lighter style of being?

Lizard: Unfolds your shadows through dream energy. Opens you up to the possibilities of sensitivity and detachment. Look for what may be lurking in those shadows. What have you not yet brought into full consciousness? It will help you into openness. Look for the symbols to help you see into your unknowns.
Ask yourself: Am I being overly sensitive, or not sensitive enough? Am I listening with my knowingness over the perceptions of others? Am I open to the possibilities of objective detachment and new awarenesses?

Mouse: The details of the present. Are you putting life in specific detailed boxes, where there is no room for change or growth? Are you afraid to reach out into the unknown? Look carefully at the now. What is out of order, from a holistic perspective? What is in order? Study the details and then expand to the whole picture. Do not get stuck in detail, but rather reach out past your comfort zone and see what happens.
Ask yourself: Am I neglecting the necessities of life? Am I getting overwhelmed with the business of life and loosing my focus on what is truly important?

Owl: Wisdom and mystery. The seeker of inner truth and knowledge. Owl may be telling you to gather your intuitive self and look beyond the surface of your life situations, the people in your life, etc. and see what is real. Owl helps you see the total truth. Look for signs or symbols to aid in this journey of truth seeking.
Ask yourself: Am I honoring myself for seeing and hearing the truths behind the words, for using my inner eyes to look through the darkness?

Quail: Protection. Easily spots danger and then confront it loudly and clearly. It teaches mindful and direct action in regards to irritations and predicaments in life.
Ask yourself: Am I looking directly at the dilemmas in my life? Am I sensitively and promptly acting on them?

Rabbit: Represents sensitivity, intuition, and the ability to make leaps. What are you afraid of? It may be time to analyze the fears before they consume you. If this has begun, ask why you are holding on to the fears. Remember the law of attraction: like attracts like. What you believe you become. If you fear something you draw it to you. Go into a safe space, search your fears and then rest.

Ask yourself: Am I aware of the signs around me and the movement needed within my life? Where am I being asked to take a leap of faith?

Raven: Bearer of magic. Represents a change in consciousness or thought. Accept change as it shows. The raven shows you that you are ready. You do not need to understand or even know what the change is this part of the magic of raven. It unfolds if you allow it to have natural flow.

Ask yourself: Am I accepting the magic into my life? Am I bringing light and new awareness into darkened areas of my life?

Roadrunner: Represents mental speed and agility. Represents the ability to change directions with spontaneity, without planning or labored analysis.

Ask yourself: Am I able to think quickly on my feet or is my thought process slow and habitual? Is my creative mind balanced enough that I can think quickly and change directions skillfully?

Snake: Represents rebirth, resurrection and the shedding of old skin. It helps you develop and see your own wholeness. Creativity and sexuality are also associated with the snake.

Ask yourself: What do I need to shed so as to accept wholeness? Where is there a need for a new life? Am I striking out, or not striking out where I feel an impulse for change? What needs to be healed in my life? Where is there a surge of creativity or sexuality asking to be freed and utilized?

Spider: Teaches about self creation and how responsible you are for the creations. It may be time to open to your own creativity. Or is it time to look at what "tangled webs" you may have already woven. Is it time to sort things out? Are things in perfect order? Look at where life is to see your creations and where they fit in your eternal plan.

Ask yourself: Am I balanced in my life? Do I realize that everything I do now affects my weaving of the future? Am I moving towards a single focus or going off in scattered directions?

Stewardship

Those officially charged with the stewardship of the sacred sites and ruins in this area have pledged to honor and care for the land. We can be honorary stewards by being respectful of where we travel, picking up any garbage we see, regardless if we are the one who left behind the refuse, and by teaching others what we know about respecting the land through our words and example.

The following are requests from the stewards as well as the residents of Sedona. We are presenting their requests because we want to work in cooperation with them.

Please Do:
1. Enter these areas in a spirit of respectfulness for the land, the ancientness of any artifacts, and for the significance they hold for many people.

2. Stay on existing trails and obey signs. Where trails are unclear, walk carefully. The vegetation is sensitive and does not readily grow back.

3. Be careful, and avoid climbing or standing near ledges. The rock is soft, often loose and may give way easily.

4. Take time for quiet reflection and enjoy the scenic, environmental, and spiritual beauty of these areas. If others are meditating at a site when you arrive, be respectful and keep your voices low.

5. Report if you see people vandalizing sites or starting fires as soon as possible. 24-hour line (602) 526-0600.

Please Don't:
1. Start fires of any kind at the sites, even candles. Fire can destroy prehistoric organic materials, ruin the dating potential of artifacts, and damage rock art by covering it with soot.

2. Take home any rocks or rock fragments, natural vegetation, or cut standing trees or tree limbs.

3. Leave medicine wheels or alters you built in the sacred sites. Disassemble them when you are done and leave the environment in its natural state.

4. Draw or scratch graffiti on rocks or cliff faces. Do not touch petroglyphs. Oil from your hands can cause deterioration of the drawings.

5. Camp or sleep in ruins, or dig or remove artifacts in a site. Do not add anything (offerings) to a site. This contaminates cultural deposits that are important for scientific tests used by archaeologists in reconstructing past environments and dietary information about the people who occupied these sites.

Definitions

Chakras: Energy points within the body. They help us create interaction with ourselves and other people. Refer to diagram on page   for more information.

Channeling: The process of communication with non-physical beings, often referred to as spirit or invisible helpers. The person channeling is referred to as the channel or medium.

Clairvoyance: The ability to see with your inner psychic eyes.

Clairaudience: The ability to hear with your inner psychic ears.

Clairsentience: The ability to feel with your inner psychic senses.

Commitment: A defined, chosen focus that one holds so that change and movement can occur.

Crystals: A rock formation with six sides that comes to a point on one or both ends. It is often clear in color and is an energy tool that helps gather more information. They are also able to enhance healing. They help one to focus.

Dreams: The night language of the heart. Refer to page   for more information on dreams in reference to the vortexes.

Emotions: An already established attitude or belief about what is occurring at a particular moment. It expresses itself through emoting.
> **Examples of emotion** - loneliness, fear, resentment, sorrow, jealousy, rage, exhilaration.

Energy: Eternal life force in everyone and everything.
> **Electric** - Physical, moving, active, releasing kind of energy. Masculine in nature.
> **Magnetic** - Intuitive, inner, quiet, sensitive kind of energy. Feminine in nature.
> **Electro-Magnetic** - A blend of electric and magnetic energy.

Feeling: A natural expression of the body. A natural informational system used to connect the mind, body and spirit. Easiest way to identify a feeling would be by expressing yourself in the following way, "I am feeling angry, sick, happy, sad, etc."
> **Examples of feeling** - fatigue, hunger, angry, sad, happy, numb, scared.

Goddess: The expression of the feminine aspects of Godliness.

Healing: A process that returns the body to balance, the mind to peace and the spirit to connection.

Higher Self: Our observer or silent witness. It looks at things from the highest and most loving perspective. It is very objective and factual and the emissary between self and God.

Intuition: A keen, natural knowingness or insight. Sensitivity to feelings and energy. It is a perception of truth or fact independent of any reasoning process.

Journal: A personal written record of your thoughts, feelings and insights. It also offers you the opportunity to tap into unconscious insights.

Kundalini: A profound, healing force that creates a consciousness changing experience. It rises from the base of the spine to the top of your head and back down.

Male/Female Energy: Each person hold both energies within themselves. A balance of both is required for a person to obtain wholeness.
> **Attributes of male energy** - goal and action oriented, manifesting, doing, logical, protective, giving energy.
> **Attributes of female energy** - receptivity, being, creating, flowing, intuitive, nurturing, expressive through feelings and symbols, knowing.

Medicine Wheel: A symbolic wheel of life that connects different aspects of a person. Usually made of stones and divided into four quadrants with the cardinal directions at the head of each quadrant.

Meditation: The process of quieting the mind and body so as to receive information, guidance, knowledge. It can bring about a sense of inner peace and a reduction of stress and a connection to spirit. It is a state of receptivity.

Past Lives: Previously lived earth experiences.

Pinnacle: Regarding the vortexes in Sedona, they are the spires of rock that stretch up into the sky. Often seen in magnetic energy vortexes.

Psychic Experience: The focusing of intuitive energy to be used in specific ways.

Reincarnation: The process where your soul chooses another life experience to further its earth knowledge.

Sedona: A town in Northern Arizona known and respected as a center of great transformation and healing. It is surrounded by at least four major vortexes. Originally named after a settler named Sedona Schnebly. The word Sedona is often used to refer to the vortexes in the area.

Spirit Guides: Non-physical beings who have chosen to assist us with our earth walk through teaching, guiding and supporting us.

Subconscious: The storehouse of past information.

Third Eye: Located in the 6th chakra, in the center of the forehead. It is the doorway into your intuitive, clairvoyant or psychic abilities.

Transformation: A process that creates permanent change in one's life. Metamorphosis. The changing from one form to another; such as a caterpillar to a butterfly.

Unconscious: Information not yet known to our conscious awareness.

Symbol: An image or concept that represents something unknown or deeper than what is obvious. Example - Upon seeing a rose, you wonder what a rose means and why is it showing itself to you at this moment. A symbol presents itself to find the deeper meaning.

Vortex: A unique flow of energy, usually a spiraling kind of motion. If it is electric in nature, it comes up from the earth out to the sky, and is honored for its transformational ability. A magnetic vortex flows from the tops of the rocks or pinnacles down to the earth. The magnetic vortexes are often honored for their ability to open up the unconscious.

Courthouse Rock

References

Buffalo Woman Comes Singing, Brooke Medicine Eagle, Ballantine Books, New York, 1991

In the Shadow of the Shaman, Amber Wolfe, Llewellyn Publications, St. Paul, Mn., 1989

Living Your Dreams, Sharon Marer, M.S., Self Published, 1982

Sedona, Sacred Earth, Nicholas R. Mann, ZIVAH Publishers, Prescott, Az. 1989/1991

Sedona, Psychic Energy Vortexes, Dick Sutphen, Valley of the Sun Publisher, Malibu, Ca., 1986

Sedona Guide, Day Hiking & Sightseeing Arizona's Red Rock Country, Steve Krause & Teresa Henkle, Pinyon Publishing Co., 1991

Sedona Hikes, 2nd Edition, Richard & Sherry Mangum, Hexagon Press, Flagstaff, Az., 1994

The Ancient Ruins of Sedona, Hoyt Johnson, Sedona Magazine, Sedona, Az., 1993

The Mystery of Sedona, The New Age Frontier, Tom Dongo, Hummingbird Publisher, Sedona, Az., 1988

Understanding Yourself Through Your Chakras, Shirley Piwonski, Sources of Light, 1991

Wheels of Life, Anodea Judith, Llewellyn Publications, St. Paul, Mn., 1987

About the Authors...

Sharon Marer has a Master's Degree in Counseling Psychology. She has travelled the Northwest presenting workshops and training in the areas of personal and spiritual growth. She has shared her knowledge from college classrooms to corporate meeting rooms. Along with writing and training, she maintains a private practice in Portland, Oregon, where she offers individual and group consultations.

Sharon is the author of a booklet, *"Living Your Dreams."* It is a guidebook for integrating dreams into your daily life. She is currently writing a book titled *"Ordinary Heros,"* a collection of stories and teachings that create a blueprint for spiritual living.

Shirley Piwonski is a minister and trance channel, who has been working with spirit for over twelve years. She has worked with many organizations, churches and bookstores in the Pacific Northwest. Her gift includes the ability to channel personal spirit teachers. Currently, along with writing and presenting workshops, she holds weekly classes as well as private sessions wherein one is able to visit with spirit for a more personal touch.

Shirley has written a book titled *"Introduction To Spirit Communication"* to help people understand how to sit with spirit, and *"Understanding Yourself Through Your Chakras."* She has also published several workbooks and booklets that focus on spiritual growth.

Together, Sharon and Shirley facilitate transformational journeys in Sedona. Each journey has a specific theme and purpose pertinent to the fast moving, changing moments that are upon us. For more information about specific journeys call or write the publisher.

Index

A
Airport Mesa v, 3, 14, 15, 21-29, 32-34, 39, 40, 50
Artifacts 195, 196
Animals 60, 61, 74, 115, 117, 124, 158, 187

B
Back O'Beyond i, 69, 75
Balance 13, 16, 19, 35, 56, 86, 95, 98, 99, 101, 102, 104, 105, 117, 120, 123, 125, 152, 155, 157, 160, 161, 180, 181, 190, 193, 194, 198, 199
Bell Rock 4, 5, 7, 13, 14, 18, 19, 22, 45-53, 55-62, 68, 144
Boynton Pass Rd. 8
Breathing 19, 23, 28, 30, 55, 57, 61, 78 178, 189

C
Capital Butte 3
Chakras vi, 16, 17, 34-38, 57-59, 159-162, 179-181, 197, 200, 202, 203
Cathedral Rock v, 4-6, 13, 15, 16, 19, 22, 24, 67-75, 87, 89, 93-98, 100-106, 144, 177
Ceremonies 12, 156
Chimney Rock 3

Clairvoyance 121, 181, 197
Cleansing 26, 34, 38, 48, 49, 58, 61, 103, 107, 159, 190
Coffeepot Rock 3
Color 34-39, 58, 59, 70, 74, 77, 79, 84, 85, 108, 154-162, 165, 171, 185, 197
  black ii, 155, 158
  blue 37, 38, 84, 85, 160, 171, 179, 180
  indigo 38, 160, 179, 181
  orange 35, 85, 160, 179, 180
  red 34, 35, 46, 84, 85, 154, 158, 160, 179, 180
  purple 38, 160, 179, 181
  white 59-61, 143, 156, 158
  yellow 36, 46, 84, 85, 157, 158, 160, 179, 180
Commitment i, 33, 71, 98, 100, 197
Cottonwood 3, 6, 8
Courthouse Rock 4, 7, 22, 48, 201

D
Dolphins i, 67, 68, 83, 86-89, 106-108, 189

Dreams vi, 17, 18, 27, 48, 132, 134, 143, 155, 171, 177, 182, 183, 185-188, 191, 197, 202, 203
Dry Creek Rd. 8

E
Eastgate 157
Enchantment Resort 8, 113, 114
Electric 12-16, 23, 27, 28, 45, 46, 120, 121, 131-133, 198, 201
Electro-Magnetic 13, 16, 113, 198
Environment 153, 154, 177, 190, 195, 196
Exercises 14, 30, 31, 55-61, 78, 83, 106, 125, 134, 150, 151, 153, 159, 163, 176

G
General Crook 12
Green rock mass 95
Goddess 51, 131, 132, 198

H
Healing 16, 19, 50, 56, 59, 61, 93-95, 103, 106, 141, 144, 180, 197-200
Hiking 52, 175, 177, 202

I
Indent 55-61
Indian 12, 115-117
Inner Knowing 72, 73, 83, 181

Intuition 16, 143, 181, 187, 192, 199

K
Kachina Woman 8, 9, 113, 114, 116, 118, 131-134, 136, 137
Kundalini 24, 199

L
Lemuria 67, 68, 83, 87, 89

M
Magnetic 12, 13, 15, 16, 70, 71, 94, 96, 113, 120, 121, 198, 200, 201
Masculine/Feminine Energy
  masculine 12, 198
  male 86, 87, 95, 101, 133, 199
  feminine 12, 69, 70, 198
  female 86, 87, 95, 101, 133, 199
Medicine Wheel 4, 22, 26, 27, 39, 115, 142, 150, 151, 153-159, 163, 166, 196, 199
Meditation vi, 18, 30, 34, 60, 61, 83, 106, 125, 159, 163, 176, 199
Movement v, 14, 21, 23, 36, 47, 48, 50, 52, 53, 59, 86, 100, 123, 144, 188, 193, 197
Munds Mt. 3

N
Night Fire 21, 24, 34, 37, 38
Northgate 156, 200, 203

O
Oak Creek 5, 7, 93, 94, 98, 102

P
Partnership 95, 98-100
Past Life 199
Petrogliphs 196
Pictures 11, 13, 23, 48, 77, 79, 94, 96, 105, 120, 171, 189
Pinnacles 15, 69, 71, 73, 78-82, 90, 108, 200, 201
Prayers iv, 9, 72, 133, 134, 136, 152, 153, 156
Psychic i, 13, 68, 117, 155, 157, 171, 197, 200, 202

R
Red Rock Crossing 5, 6, 93, 94, 102
Rebirth 51, 155, 187, 193
Rituals 12, 156
Ruins 195, 196, 202

S
Schnebly Hill 10, 11, 16, 19, 141-148, 151, 153, 159, 166, 167, 200
Schnebly Hill Rd. 10
Sinagua 12
Southgate 151, 152, 154
Space Brothers i, 48, 52

Spires 71, 95, 101, 104, 114, 131, 200
Spiraling Energy 13, 30, 45, 142, 201
Stewardship 195
Symbols 9, 15, 16, 18, 23, 28, 30, 31, 73, 77, 79, 105, 115, 118, 120, 121, 124-126, 131, 134, 142, 154-157, 171, 182, 185, 191, 192, 199, 201

T
Third Eye 38, 67, 121, 165, 181, 200
Trail ii, iii, vi, 4-10, 21, 45, 46, 70, 93-97, 100, 101, 114, 116, 117, 122, 143, 163, 195

V
Vision v, vi, 9, 12, 27, 68, 89, 124, 147, 181
Verde Valley Rd. 5, 99

W
Westgate 155
Wilson Mt. 3

Y
Yavapai 12